THE YOUTH EVOLUTION

*The New Approach to Focusing
The Next Generation on Success*

This Book is for

_____

Yetunde Adeshile
Award Winning Author

www.YetundeAdeshile.com
www.TheYouthEvolution.com

ISBN: 978-0-9933159-0-9

First published 2015

2nd edition

Copyright © 2015 Yetunde Adeshile. All rights reserved.

All rights reserved. Apart from any permitted use under UK copyright law, no part of this publication may be reproduced or transmitted in any form or by any means, electronic or mechanical, including photocopying, recording, or any information, storage or retrieval system, without permission in writing from the publisher or under licence from the Copyright Licensing Agency Limited. Further details of such licenses (for reprographic reproduction) may be obtained from the Copyright Licensing Agency Ltd, Saffron House, 6-10 Kirby Street, London EC1N 8TS.

Editing delivered by Apex Writing Services, apexwritingserices@gmail.com and the Raymond Aaron Group's Editing Services, 445 Apple Creek Blvd, Suite 122, Markham, Ontario, Canada, L3R 9X7

Printed in Great Britain for Yetunde Adeshile by Bell & Bain Ltd, 303 Burnfield Road, Thornliebank, Glasgow G46 7UQ

Orders: Please visit www.TheYouthEvolution.com or contact.

RJ Emmanuel Ltd
The Laindon Barn
Dunton Road
Basildon
Essex
SS13 1HJ

Ph: 01268 330120
Fax: 01268 330742

You can also order via email: enquires@rjemmanuel.com

CONTENTS

Foreword by Yemisi Akindele 7

Foreword by Raymond Aaron 9

Testimonials 11

Preface – I Have a Dream 15

Introduction: The Journey That Unleashed My Passion 18

Chapter 1: Why Should You Care About The
Next Generation? 27

Chapter 2: Youth and the Evolution 37

Chapter 3: Youth Influencers 47

Chapter 4: Your Children, Your Future 61

Chapter 5: The New Approach to Focusing
Youths for Success 71

Chapter 6: Focus for Spiritual Success 81

Chapter 7: Focus for Academic Success 89

Chapter 8: Focus for Career Success 99

Chapter 9: Focus for Business Success 105

Chapter 10: Success - No Matter What! 113

Chapter 11: The Evolution Is In Your Hands 121

The Next Chosen Generation (TNCG) Events 130
About the Author 132
Acknowledgments 134
Bibliography 137
Recommended Resources 139
Useful Sites 140

DEDICATION

*This book is dedicated to both my late parents
Rev. (Chief) E O Ashamu
and Rev. (Mrs) Caroline Bola Ashamu.*

*Thank you both for your investments in me.
You will always remain in my heart.*

May your souls continue to rest in perfect peace.

DISCLAIMER

Although the author and publisher have made every effort to ensure that the information in this book was correct at press time, the author and publisher do not assume and hereby disclaim any liability to any party for any loss, damage, or disruption caused by errors or omissions, whether such errors or omissions result from negligence, accident, or any other cause.

Some names and identifying details have been changed to protect the privacy of individuals.

FOREWORD

Firstly I want to appreciate the effort that has gone into this book by all the contributors. Yetunde Adeshile is a true inspiration to this generation, especially for the effort she has made in putting the content of this book together. The Youth Evolution sets out to be a game changer for the next generation of parents, leaders, community workers and youths in the society.

I was privileged to meet the acquaintance of Yetunde at an event where I was guest speaker on the topic of Education a few years ago. Since then I have seen Yetunde transform her children and herself to achieve greater things.

When Yetunde told me about this book, just the title alone got my attention. When we got into a discussion about the content of the book, we were there discussing for hours whilst standing. We didn't realise the time, this can be expected as we both share a passion to see the next generation succeed in life.

As the founder and CEO of High Achievers Academy (the award winning supplementary Tutoring), I have the experience and passion for helping young people achieve academic success in life. High Achievers Academy has a high success rate in preparing children for admission into top independent schools in the UK including Harrow, Eton, Wycombe Abbey et al. High Achievers also supported a pupil obtain the £200k Peter Beckwith scholarship to attend Harrow School in 2010 which was televised on Channel 4.

In 2013, I was part of the team that spearheaded an initiative with Britain's top universities which encouraged minority ethnic young people to consider a future at Oxford and Cambridge Universities following a campaign led by Labour's former higher education minister David Lammy. For the last several years, I have been privileged to make positive impact to the lives of the next generation both nationally and internationally.

The Youth Evolution book has been written at a time when the world is in great need to inspire the next generation to focus for their success. This book does not only offer practical advice to parents, teachers, leaders and mentors of the next generation, it is also inspirational and sets out to instil a desire for youths to succeed. Something compelling about this book is that once you have read it, you will come to the realisation that success is truly achievable by all. The possible "knowledge gaps" that could be holding the next generation back from success are revealed in this book.

The saying goes thus, 'information is power' but how many people get this information and turn it to power? This brilliant woman received the information that not only transformed her children's lives but hers; hence we're reading this book now. As a result of this book, lives will be transformed and destinies fulfilled. It is an honour to be a part of this book and I look forward to reading the second volume in the near future.

Yemisi Akindele
Founder and CEO High Achievers
Award Winning Supplementary Tutoring

FOREWORD

Being a parent in today's world is the greatest role that anyone will play in their entire life. Teachers, community and world leaders are also major influencers that support the outcome of every child. Therefore, we all have a great responsibility in raising the next generation. The current evolution presents us with challenges for raising the next generation and focusing them on success. We need to support youths in order for them to be successful in life, as this is crucial to the future of our world.

Over the last few years, I have travelled all over the world teaching and coaching people from multicultural backgrounds on success and investment; and how to achieve powerful goal setting strategies using life management tools that dramatically change people's lives for the better. I have also coached people on writing and publishing their books using my 10-10-10 programme.

I am committed to helping people achieve what they want in this lifetime and I have had the privilege to help hundreds of thousands of people around the world achieve their dreams with the wisdom I have received from my mentors and coaches.

As a parent that cares deeply about his children and their success in life, I am so thrilled about the contents of *The Youth Evolution.*

The contents of this book, provides information that will help parents, teachers, community leaders, religious institutions and today's leaders on building success for the next generation.

Yetunde's passions to see the next generation achieve success no matter what has been clearly demonstrated through the contents of this book. She presents simple and practical precepts that you and I can apply so that we can become focused on the success of the next generation.

Reading *The Youth Evolution* may produce a profound feeling of excitement that will enable you to make full use of the opportunities available to you and the next generation. This book is definitely a manual for life that should be passed down to future generations to come.

As I reviewed the chapters and noted the clarity of the content, I was especially impressed by the way information was presented and the ideology contained in each chapter.

I challenge you to pay careful attention to the contents of what Yetunde presents in this informative, inspirational and transformational book. Consume the wisdom on the pages of this book and you will discover what it really takes to achieve success for you and your next generation. The support solutions presented by Yetunde are highly recommended, especially as these have now become the new way of life for successful people all over the world.

Congratulations and thank you, Yetunde, for sharing your experience, desire, passion and knowledge in order for us to be informed about the youth evolution and this new approach.

Read this book with an open heart and see the results that it will present to you.

Raymond Aaron
New York Times Best-Selling Author
www.2dayTycoon.com

Raymond Aaron is the author of *Branding Small Business for Dummies and Double Your Income Doing What You Love*, besides many other bestselling books. He is known as the #1 success and investment coach, teaching people just like you how to use his goal-setting strategies to change your life.

TESTIMONIALS

"This book is a must read for all parents and those aspiring to become parents. It is recommended for Pastors and teachers so that they can be relevant in helping the youth in their churches and schools. The information and knowledge derived from this book is bigger than the size of the book itself. It is a book that must be read over and over again as your children transition from one stage to another. The book is recommended to all who want to provide their children with adequate support as they grow from one stage of life to another. I highly recommend this book for all parents."

Pastor Thomas Aderounmu
RCCG The Fountain

"As a successful businessman and entrepreneur, I wholeheartedly recommend Yetunde's book, *The Youth Evolution*. Yetunde's passion for changing the way we view, treat and nurture today's youths in our society is not only galvanising and motivating, but also a crucial part of the process for making sure the future generation achieves success. Having met Yetunde on a number of occasions, her passion for making a difference to our community is both refreshing and inspiring. This book is an absolute must-read!"

Richard McMunn
International Businessman and Entrepreneur

"Excellent practical advice to all families, especially those just starting out. The Youth Evolution authored by Yetunde Adeshile is a major benefit to all who are in the position of raising the next generation. It offers honest advise which is evidenced by the author's experience. Even if you and your next generation are currently on track for success, this book is still highly recommended. It contains so much valuable advice with content that you may not already be aware of."

Gerry Roberts
International Bestselling Author of The Millionaire Mind-set& Founder/President of Black Card Books

"Excellent! Excellent! Excellent Book!

I am very grateful for this God-inspired communication tool for bridging the generational gap, particularly between parents / caregivers and their children as they transition through life. As parents we need the tools for reaching out to our children at different stages in their lives. The way we were raised is not necessarily the appropriate way to raise our children. They were either born or live in a different society / environment and live in an information age which is sure to continue to accelerate. The book does not only raise awareness but it will inspire all parents / caregivers and youth leaders to change and find the appropriate means of communicating and helping children and youths of today. I recommend this book to all people and institutions that work with youth. parents / cares and youth organisations, churches and learning establishments. I equally recommend the coaching services run by the author."

Pastor John Addison
Christian Family Centre
Elim Pentecostal Church, Laindon, Essex

"The book is very well written, not too technical and is a practical tool for all parents. I could not help but reminisce about my childhood days and what went through my mind.

Regardless of your generation, the book is very informative. It contains lots of interesting facts about the different generations and different behaviours. I like the fact that our spirituality is the base of every advice given. The spiritual foundation that our father gave us has played a large role on our formative years and a great source of encouragement for our next generation."

Titiloye Ashamu
Creative Director Ethnikologie (NIG) LTD

"This book demonstrates that anyone can create a successful life. It offers practical advice to help the next generation to achieve their goals. Well done, Yetunde!"

Eanas El Sheakh
Educator & Youth Coach – Abu Dhabi-UAE

"Someone once said that "Christianity is one generation away from extinction so we have to make sure we look after the children." I am sure the same can be said for society as a whole.

Young people are our adults of tomorrow and without a firm foundation they will not survive the challenges of life. Yetunde brings up a very important point; how can we expect our young people to live purposeful lives if we do not first show them the way? The old adage of "do what I say and not what I do" no longer holds value as young people learn from what they see and experience.

Yetunde's use of a personal example is a powerful reminder that as adults we need to be the beacon of light that leads the way and this is true whatever your personal belief or religious connection."

Carole Pyke
CEO Words that Deliver

"If you are contemplating youth coaching then this is the book for you! Yetunde uses real life experiences to explore the questions we often ask ourselves with regard to young people today. Understanding our youth in the present day context of an ever-changing and cross-cultural society, is daunting in itself. This book helps one to find balance, manage expectations and to operate on common ground by achieving mutual respect, while dealing with young people's education and life challenges."

Karen Small
Author, Poet, Public Speaker and Creative Coach

"I would recommend that you read Yetunde's book *The Youth Evolution*. The book is practical, inspiring and motivational. Yetunde presents a valuable way that coaching can be applied in order to focus the next generation on success in different areas of their life and throughout their transitional phases."

Naval Kumar
Award Winning Author
www.navalkumar.com

"Wow!!! This book is definitely a must read. Yetunde's passion to see the next generation achieve success in life is demonstrated in the context of this book. She has been through challenges as a youth and she clearly wants to use her experience to help the next generation succeed in life. Read, learn and apply the methods within *The Youth Evolution*."

Vishal Morjaria
Award Winning Author, Transformational Speaker and Coach

PREFACE – I HAVE A DREAM

"If you want to succeed you must have vision, desire, goal, focus and a belief in yourself that you can achieve success."
Yetunde Adeshile

Like Martin Luther King Jr., I also have a dream. My dream is to see this generation succeed in life through the application of focused minds. However, most of the time when I think about this dream I often ask myself, how many people have shared the same dream for themselves and for their next generation? This leads me to ask the following questions:

- Do you know what success means?
- Do you want success for yourself and your next generation?
- Do you know how to achieve success?

If I am to ask 20 different people for their definition of success, I'm sure I would more than likely get different answers. This is simply because success has a different meaning for everyone, or at least to those who have actually thought about what success means to them.

The word success can be linked to the amount of money you have, the relationships you have, your spiritual enlightenments, your assets, living in the present or it could be a combination of two or more of these.

For the purpose of this book, I will use the definition of success taken from the Oxford Dictionary, which states

"Success (the opposite of failure) is the accomplishment of an aim or objective."

This, in simple terms, means that for you to be considered successful, you would have achieved a desired aim or objective. Without an initial aim or objective, there would be nothing to achieve and therefore success cannot be said to have been achieved.

If you understand success to be as defined above, ask yourself the following questions:

- Do you know what success you want for yourself and the next generation?
- Do you believe you can achieve your desired success?
- What gives you the confidence that you can achieve your success?
- Have you set goals that you can measure and celebrate once achieved?

It is one thing to know what success is, want it and plan for it; and it is another thing to achieve the vision or the goals that you desire. Achieving your goals in life is what makes you successful. Apart from the vision, goal and desire to be successful, you need to have the drive/motivation and focus required to achieve your end result in order to attain success. This is the success that you have defined for yourself, as no one else can define it for you.

To be focused means you need to concentrate on something in particular and keeping that thing in view until you achieve the expected result. Whatever your goal is, you must keep it as your central point of attention in order to achieve it.

Challenges Presented by lack of Vision

The challenges that we have with youths in this present day, may have been derived from their lack of vision or desire to be successful. The next generation may also not have the self-confidence or self-belief that they need in this present day because they have not been nurtured with this purpose in mind.

You will find that some young people know what they want, but are at a disadvantage because they do not have access to the resources they need to acquire it. Some do not know what they want but the skills and talents that they naturally use can point them in the right direction. Unfortunately, if there is no one to take note or provide appropriate guidance, they may miss their boat of opportunity.

The Youth Evolution presents information and possible solutions to the challenges that may be experienced by the next generation, which can distract or potentially prevent them from being successful in life. The possible solutions offered in this book provide a new approach that should be implemented in order to encourage the next generation to remain focused on their success.

The next generation need you, the previous generation, to pay more attention to their development in order for them to birth the success within them.

Yetunde Adeshile

INTRODUCTION

The Journey that unleashed my passion

It's Saturday the 17th of March, 2012.

I'm in church finalising the programme for the weekend's Women's Conference which was about to commence an hour later. The programme concluded and it's now time to get it checked by Pastor (Mrs) Elizabeth Aderounmu, President of the Good Women Fellowship at RCCG The Fountain.

I meet with Pastor (Mrs) Aderounmu in her office and as we are working through the programme, Pastor Thomas Aderounmu (My Pastor) walks in and sits opposite the both of us. We conclude the programme and Pastor T Aderounmu starts a conversation regarding the programme with us. Then he says, "Sister Yetunde, I have a request to make of you." Looking a bit worried, I am thinking, what could Pastor want me to do for him today?

"Yes sir," I replied.

"The Youth Pastor will be leaving the church as he has gotten a job opportunity in the US," he continues.

Right now I'm thinking - great for the youth pastor, but what has this got to do with me.

Pastor continues, "I would like you to take over the role from him". My laptop almost drops from my hands, I am thinking -you've got the wrong person. No way! I can't do that. No! No!! No!!! Pastor T Aderounmu continues talking about the youth church and some of the challenges they have and I just remain silent, staring at him blankly. Thinking, surely Pastor knows he's talking to the wrong person, right?

Pastor (Mrs) Aderounmu must be feeling or hearing my thoughts, because as I am about to open my mouth to let them both know

Introduction: The Journey That Unleashed My Passion

that they've got the wrong person, she stops me.

"Sister Yetunde, don't talk now, just go and pray about it and get back to us," she says, patting my arms.

"Yes, pray about it and let me know by next week, because the current youth pastor will be leaving in the next couple of weeks and you will need a hand over period," agrees Pastor T Aderounmu. Hello!! A couple of weeks???

I prayed about it, as advised and God led me to take on the role.

This, of course, is not the beginning of my story. Looking back, I realise that God used this role to remind me of my purpose in life, thus enabling me fulfil my heart's desire, which the challenges of life have made inconsequential. For many years prior to this conversation, I had been interested in helping individuals younger than myself to achieve their full potential by becoming successful in life. However, the idea of getting a job had been embedded in my belief system. I went after getting a secure office job whilst seeking to help youths became a secondary activity.

At the age of 19, I started to serve as the youth leader in church and maintained the position for about 5 years. Even when I was no longer the leader, I remained an active member. I then served in the children's church and I had the opportunity to work with children from the age of 0-18 or until they went to University. I found myself providing some sort of support to the younger people in church, especially as I had been through the whole educational process, this positioned me to provide them with experienced mentoring and coaching. At work, I had signed up to becoming a mentor to younger or new employees joining the company. Prior to this, I was already providing this support to those that needed it in the organisation outside company formalities.

In 2008, I signed up to be a STEM Ambassador for UK schools. This role provides me the opportunity to go into primary and secondary schools in and around the UK to deliver motivational/

career related talks to young people and occasionally helping young people to prepare for their first jobs.

Over the last few years, several people have contacted me for parenting and youth related advice. This made me realise that there is a real issue with raising youths in today's world. Youths, like their parents and teachers, have issues; and it sometimes seems as though the youths have been left to their own device. As a result of this, some families and communities are being negatively impacted. With this thought in mind, something began to stir inside me. I didn't quite know what it was, but I knew I wanted to be a part of the solution to these highlighted issues, that are presented to me on a regular basis.

One morning in January 2014, I had just completed my morning devotion when my friend David rang me to say the usual Happy New Year greetings. Our conversation slipped into the following.

David: "What would you do, if God gave you £10million to spend on anything you want?"

Me: Wow. That's a pretty random question for the New Year I thought to myself. "I don't know, why do you ask?

David: "Think, what would you do?"

Me: "Actually, I would purchase a place like the KICC's land of wonders. Have you seen it?"

David: "No, I haven't seen it. What would you use it for?"

Me: "When, I was about 10 years younger I wanted to purchase a place similar to the land of wonders so that children and youths could come for holiday camps there. The place would be a place where they can be themselves, learn, develop, transform and grow." I would still run my current business though. I have worked too hard to let it go."

David: "Yetunde, you should be working full-time with the youths. You see, only a person that truly cares about the youth would want something like that. Anyway, you know what the Bible says in Habakkuk 2:2 "And the LORD answered me, and said, write the vision, and make it plain upon tables, that he may run that readeth it."

I meditated on this Bible passage for a couple of weeks and then one day I decided to write my vision for working full time with youths.

A couple of months later my husband and I attended the TD Jakes Pastors and Leaders International Conference at the Orange County Convention Centre in Florida USA. We were amongst a large crowd of this international audience. Upon entering the auditorium for the first time, I remember feeling overwhelmed at the crowd and the spiritual atmosphere. I was convinced that the conference was going to present me with life-transforming messages.

During the conference I was fortunate to achieve a certificate in ministry leadership and executive management, which was an added bonus.

Bishop TD Jakes opened the conference with a ministration titled *The Instinct to Shift.* Bishop talked about a time when he was out ministering in Mississippi and he had been loaned a manual car by his host. He talked about how he found it challenging to change the gears of the car because he was not used to driving a stick shift (manual car). Bishop drove the car in gear 1 for longer than he should have, which gave the car a grinding sound. He then said that the sound the car was making indicated that there was something wrong with the car. At that moment he said to the audience "Isn't this how you sometimes feel. You feel stuck and you are grinding on one spot." For that moment, I thought to myself, that's exactly how I feel. I couldn't move forward or backward. I'm just grinding on the same spot. I spent the rest of the ministration saying to myself "My God that's me, he's talking to me." I had attended the conference knowing there was something that wasn't quite right. I felt that there was something that I should be doing but I wasn't. I felt that I had been stuck for many years with wanting to help the next generation, but couldn't actually do what I wanted, or that what I was doing wasn't doing enough. It's as if over the years my desire to see younger people succeed in life had slipped away from my radar. Although, I was serving in the youth church, mentoring in schools as a STEM Ambassador or school mentor, I came to the realization that my purpose and destiny was to help the next generation achieve success and I needed a platform that would allow me to realise my vision to make positive global impact in the life of the next generation.

On day two of the conference, Dr. Cynthia James, talked about how we are called to lead the future and how we had been strategically placed by God to lead wherever we go. Then I heard her say, all you need is a little "pak". Dr. James explained that a "pak" is a Hebrew word, meaning a little drop. As I heard her say "a little pak", my mind began to wonder, "How am I to take a little pak?" I'm already serving as the youth pastor in church, I'm already volunteering in schools across London? What else am I supposed to do? "Dr. James, you don't understand there's something stirring inside of me. I don't even know what it is and you're saying start with a little step". I said to myself. "A little step for what? I can't take a little step for what I don't know. O God help me."

At the conference, Bishop TD Jakes had his new book *Instincts* on pre-order. I of course ordered the book, as the title was aligned to his opening ministration.

My husband and I returned to the UK, but life never remained the same for either of us.

Once the book arrived, I read it within days. Upon opening the inside cover of the book, I read "We know there's a bigger, elephant-sized life out there waiting for us, but uncertainty and fear keep us locked in our routines, contained in the cage of

Introduction: The Journey That Unleashed My Passion

conformity. We watch others excel as they listen to their own instincts rather than please others. Yet we ignore the urgent message whispering within us, intrigued by its insistence but afraid to act on its information." Dr. TD Jakes, *Instincts*, 2014. This reading was too applicable to me, so that was me glued to the book until the end. By the time I completed the book, I had more clarity on my purpose and I became more confident to act upon my instincts. Reading the book also motivated and made me more determined to follow my instincts. My instinct was what had been stirring in me over several years, and even as far back as when I was 19. With this realization and determination to do something about my instincts, I shared the content of the book with my husband who also had something stirring in him for over a decade. I managed to persuade him that we had to pursue our instincts no matter what, as we run the risk of not fulfilling destiny if we don't. Apart from that, life had become uncomfortable and almost unbearable with us talking about our dreams without taking a step to realize them.

Though I was worried and still nervous about proceeding with our instincts, we proceeded fearfully as recommended in one of Joyce Meyer's audio teaching *"Overcoming Fear with Faith"*. We prayed to God for him to walk with us as we started out on our journey to fulfilling destiny. We proceeded with a little pak for what we both had in us for many, many years. My husband's little pak lead to the release of his own CD album (Kakaki – Album Tunes of Praise: www.KakakiTones.com) two months after we arrived back in the UK. This has now exposed him to many opportunities nationally and internationally. The little pak that I took, lead me to establishing The Next Chosen Generation (TNCG).

TNCG is an organisation that offers mentoring and coaching for youths in-order to support them in realising their full potential and focus on success. Workshops and seminars are delivered in school, universities, corporate organisation, charity organisations, religious groups, community organisation and private groups. To find out more, please visit the web site at: www.TheNextChosenGeneration.com

One Saturday afternoon, I was delivering a TNCG session on relationships. In this session, the group decided to focus on relationships with parents, and how to improve these relationships through communication. I was actually shocked, because I thought being youths, they would have preferred to focus on peer group relationships. During the session, one of the coachee's asked "Can you please speak to my parents?, because all that we have just done and discussed here today won't work in my house." To my surprise, others in the session agreed with him. They all felt it was all good that I had helped them to identify better ways of communicating with their parents, but they felt that their parents may not give them a positive response because they are to set in their ways. Another contribution was "Parents need to try and understand us as well." This got me thinking, especially as I've noticed similar thoughts and questions from other youth forums where the topic has been based on love and relationships. I am often asked by young people to speak to their parents, but I always encourage them to find ways to address issues with those concerned by themselves. This is because I believe doing so will give them an opportunity to come up with the best approach to present the matters with their parents, families or other parties that are involved in their lives. This is also more likely to achieve a better result than if I got involved in what I consider to be a very private matter.

Following this particular TNCG mentoring and coaching seminar, I couldn't stop thinking about how to get through to the parents without jeopardising my confidentiality commitment to the group and their parents. In search of an answer to my thoughts, I decided to enrol on a Coaching within Education Diploma programme with The Coaching Academy. This programme mainly focuses on coaching youths but brings into realisation that parents, teachers and head teachers have a great influence on young people and how their beliefs are formed. It was during this programme that I realised that parents need support in raising the next generation. This realisation coupled with my desire to see the next generation succeed in all that they do, inspired me to incorporate parent coaching programmes at TNCG. These coaching sessions support parents to become more successful within their environment and role as parents. Workshops are normally delivered in corporate organisations, charity organisations, religious groups, community organisations and with private groups.

The world around us is changing every day, the new generation of youths are very different to that of the 60s, 70s, 80s and even the 90s. What young people are exposed to now is very different from what you and I were exposed to then, and all with very easy access. There are more choices, more distractions, more challenges and therefore more decisions to be made. The world for the next generation has become an ever-changing environment, with Political, Environmental, Sociological, Technological, Legal and Economic influences.

The Youth Evolution has been written to inform parents, youths, youth ministers, youth workers, schools, universities, communities and any institutions supporting the development of the next generation that there is an evolution. An evolution that cannot be stopped, changed or eradicated. An evolution that must be managed, to increase the success rate for the next generation.

This book also provides a means to empower youth, parents, religious institutions, educational institutions and local communities to embrace the concept of coaching into their teaching practices in order to support the next generation so that they can become more confident, structured and better prepared to manage the ever-evolving life challenges themselves.

The strategy presented in this book seeks to enable you to:

- Have a better understanding about the youth evolution, and what impact it has on the next generation.
- Understand the requirements for focusing the next generation on success in relation to their environment, spirituality, education, career or business opportunities

- Gain a better understanding of the UK educational stages and the laws relating to youths in the UK

- Be challenged to adapt your thinking and reasoning in order to achieve the results that you desire

- Become knowledgeable about how coaching techniques can support you to achieve success.

Chapter 1

Why should we care about the next generation?

CHAPTER 1
Why should we care about the next generation?

My mother and I had boarded the train at London Paddington. The train was heading towards Bath.

"How are you feeling about going to your new school?" asked Mum.

"Fine mum," I replied.

"You won't be called Yetunde in your new school, you'll be called Juliet," Mum said.

"Juliet! That's a nice name. Where is it from?"

"Oh it's your grandmother's name, you were named after her," Mum replied. Thrilled that I share the same name as my grandmother, I continued with my moments of joy, I watched the leaves run through the wind as the train journeyed on.

The train finally stopped at Bath Railway Station. We got off the train and entered a taxi that was to take us to our final destination - my new boarding house.

After what seemed like a long journey (I slept right through the taxi journey), the taxi pulled into the park way of a very beautiful Victorian building that was located on a quiet road and surrounded by green fields. There were no other houses in site.

As we stepped out of the car we were greeted by a middle aged couple. The man appeared to be slightly bald, he was tall and was wearing glasses. There was also a lady, who was also wearing glasses, had curly hair but was just a little taller than me. They appeared to be a nice couple.

"Good afternoon Mrs. Ashamu. Welcome to Lower Edgarley Hall boarding house for girls". (This is the junior school to Millfield

CHAPTER 1. Why Should You Care About The Next Generation?

School, Somerset, UK). "And you must be Juliet," said the man. "My name is Mr Jones and this is my wife Mrs. Jones. We are the house parents of this boarding house," Mr Jones continued.

As Mr and Mrs Jones continued in discussion with my mum, we were shown around the boarding house, which was quite big with about 10 dormitories. There was a sense of warmness and a homely atmosphere. The other girls we saw as we walked round also seemed friendly. Finally we arrive in the room for my age group. The room had eight beds in it. Beside each bed was a long brown wardrobe. Each bed area also had its own little space for movement, I guess. There are four bed spaces on each side of the room. As we walked towards the end of the room,

Mrs. Jones said, "This will be your bed, hope you like it?"

I nodded my head and gently put some of my things on the bed. My bed was, in my opinion, the best bed in the room, especially as it was located by the window. I looked round the room and felt that everything was ok.

We all walked back out to where we started the tour of the house and it wasn't until my mum was saying her good byes that reality hit me. I thought, Oh God! My mum is leaving me here on my own. She's not going to spend the night? Don't get me wrong. I knew I was going to a new school and that it was a boarding school, but this was my first experience of being away from home and I didn't expect that I would feel the way I was feeling. I was only eight years old and had just arrived in the UK from Nigeria the previous night, so I guess I might have had mixed feeling with the whole situation.

As my mum proceeded towards the taxi, I was walking with her, with a bit of hope that she might take me with her. When she realised that I was following her, she turned round, smiled and said with her gentle voice, "No darling, you're not coming with me, you will be staying here". I watched my mother go back into the taxi without me. As the taxi reversed out of the compound, I started to walk towards it with tears rolling down my eyes. When the taxi got onto the road and faced the right direction, I began to walk faster and gradually running to the end of the compound, only to see it driving off down the road. I screamed, 'Mummy! Mummy!! Until the word became very hard to say and I broke down in tears. It became obvious that my mum could no longer hear my cry; neither would the taxi be coming back. The feeling inside of me was not good. I felt rejected, upset and confused. Why was I here? Why had my mum decided to leave me here on my own? Not only was I on my own, but I soon realised that I now belonged to a minority group, whereas a few days ago, I was within the majority. So many thoughts filled my mind for weeks and months as I was left alone in my own world.

In this new world of boarding school, I had to deal with a change in environment, culture, racism, favouritism along with the growing pains of becoming a young female teenager. There really wasn't anyone to talk to. This new world meant that my parents were abroad, my sisters and brothers were all over the world with a couple of them being in the same school but facing their own personal challenges and I was surrounded by teachers who couldn't possibly understand what I was going through (that was my understanding at the time). I didn't know who to talk to about my emotional state. I didn't even know I had an emotional state.

Thankfully, the decision my parents made to take me to boarding school in the UK has worked out to my advantage. I ended up staying in the same school till I was 16 and I can honestly say that I actually enjoyed the rest of my days at boarding school. Today I can honestly say it's one of the best things that God enabled my parents to do for me. However, I know a few people that I grew up with who had a completely different experience and have negative feelings towards the time they spent in school.

Now a surviving youth who is also a parent, I ask myself and other parents the following questions?

CHAPTER 1. Why Should You Care About The Next Generation?

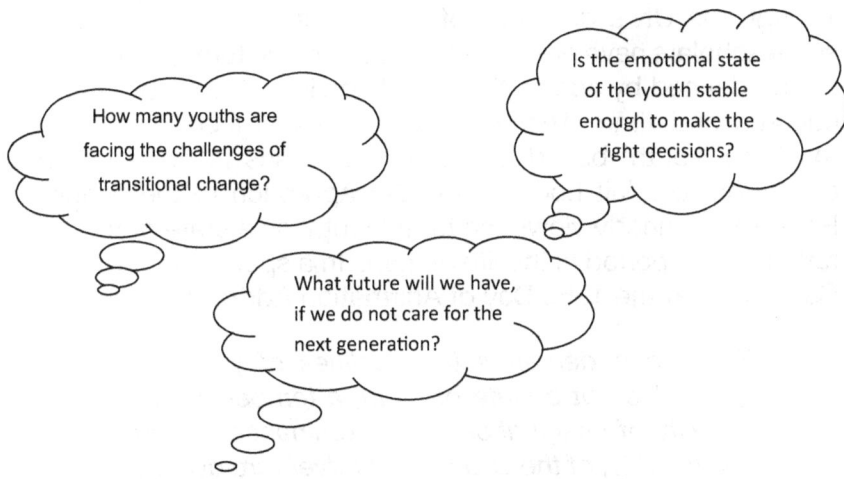

Before I can attempt to answer the above questions, I think it is worthwhile to clarify the term "youth". Some of the above will be addressed in subsequent chapters.

The term youth can be described as a transitional phase between childhood and adulthood. The United Nations Educational, Scientific and Cultural Organization (UNESCO) defined youth as a *period of transition from the dependence of childhood to the independence of adulthood and awareness of our interdependence as members of a community. Youth is a more fluid category than a fixed age-group.*

Although UNESCO considers the term youth as a category rather than an age-group, defining youths in terms of age is used especially in relation to employment and education. As such, youths may be considered to be persons between the age when they may leave compulsory education (in the UK, this is age 16), and the age at which they finds their first employment. This forms the basis for the United Nations' (UN) definition of youths, which are persons between the ages of 15 and 24 years. The definition can also be based on the definition given in the African Youth Charter where "youth" means "every person between the ages of 15 and 35 years"[1].***United Nations, 2015***

Though the UN's definition of a youth is based on age-group, some scholars have presented a case that, the term youths should not be defined by age as the use of age is varied across nations, cultures and time. These scholars have argued that defining the term 'youth' based on social processes in transition from childhood to adult hood is a better approach to the definition. Robert F. Kennedy views the term 'youth' as a state of the mind, rather than a period in the life of man. In a speech he delivered in Capetown, at the 1966 Day of Affirmation Address, he said:

> *"This world demands the qualities of youth: not a time of life but a state of mind, a temper of the will, a quality of imagination, a predominance of courage over timidity, of the appetite for adventure over the life of ease."* - **Robert Kennedy, 1966.**

The transitional phases that scholars are referring to are represented in the transition phases from child-to-adult as detailed in the table below. This is based on children developing in the UK.

Transitional Age Range	Transitional Events
Age 0 - 2	Baby. Actions are mainly based on emotions. Feelings are developed and very basic education is introduced. More children are being taken to Nursery or other form of childcare services.
Age 3 - 6	Children are transitioning from home to nursery or primary schools. They are not able to make mental choices for themselves.
Age 7 - 10	Children start to problem solve, test things out for themselves. They are moving towards the completion of their primary education and preparing for their secondary educational phase.

CHAPTER 1. Why Should You Care About The Next Generation?

Age 11 - 16	They are at the secondary phase of their education. At the beginning of this phase, they are introduced to the concept of GCSE's. By age 13 or so, they are expected to make choices about GCSE subjects and carrier choices. By age 15 they are expected to start thinking about their future more. More decisions need to be made at this stage. These include choices about A-level subjects, BTEC, IGCSE, International Baccalaureate, New School/College, 6th Form College, Work, Gap year, Apprentice. By this age children have become more independent. They are aware that they have some rights and entitlements.
Age 17 - 18/19	For those that progress along the educational path, at this stage they would have commenced their A-Levels and now looking into making University Choices based on their career path. Other options to consider at this stage includes again gap year, employment, business start-up and voluntary work abroad. As they approach the age of adulthood (age 18). They begin to gain more ground and independence. By law they are fully grown adults that can make most decisions, if not all decisions by themselves if they so wish.
Age 19 - 21+	At the beginning of this transitional phase, the young adults will be entering university (if they have chosen the academic path). Here they are presented with more choices. They would have by now chosen their degree, but within the degree there subject choices that needs to be made based on area of specialism and or interest. At the completion of the first degree other choices also need to be made. I.e. Further studies, Employment, Marriage, Business, and their Accommodation i.e. Where they are going to live.

Table 1.0: Youth Development Transitional Events
Based on scholars and Siegler R.S, Emerging Minds:
The Process of Change in Children's Thinking, 1996

My experience of working with young people, being a mother of three and having been a youth but now a responsible adult, has exposed me to some of the challenges that young people can and do face as they transition through the different stages of life. These challenges range from decision-making and solving problems to testing things and finding out solutions. They gradually have to start making decisions on their own about the choices that life presents to them as they develop into adulthood. More often at a much younger age than as young adults because there is limited support available to them.

As young people attempt to tackle these challenges based on their own understanding, some are likely to feel panic, fear, worry, and emotional-disturbance due to their limiting beliefs and possibly the relationships they may have with their parents, teachers and peers. This feeling can sometimes de-motivate or lead them to giving up and therefore they may not achieve their full potential. The Pike Syndrome suggests that children give up before they start when the right support is not available to them. We therefore need to teach them to know how to take responsibility for themselves and how to get what they want in life. There are coaching techniques that are available to support youth through their transitional phase. For coaching services, contact me at www.TheNextChosenGeneration.

Recently, I was reading a newspaper article when my attention was drawn to the article about a young lad who was 19 years old. The picture in this paper showed him carrying guns. He was carrying guns that looked like he was going out to war. The article had stated that the young man was on his way to carry out a shooting at his school. For the rest of my journey, I wondered what could have been going through the mind of this boy that he felt that this was an option for his future. Did he really understand the consequences of what he was doing? Was he aware that he could potentially get injured or killed in this process? On another day, it was a beautiful Sunday morning. As I was driving to church, I noticed a young man walking down the road with a bottle of alcohol in his hand. He looked like he hadn't slept all night. My mind wondered of with many questions all the way to church.

I don't know if it's me, but recently, I have begun to notice a lot more youths wasting time doing what they are not supposed to be doing. Some have got themselves caught up in drugs, early-aged sex (which in some cases has led to teenage pregnancy), excessive drinking, reckless driving. It's not surprising that some are now dropping out of school at a very young age with no clear direction of what they are going to do after their education.

In the 21st century that we currently live in, youths are exposed to a lot more distractions than what the youths, of say 20, 10 or even 5 years ago, had experienced. Now you will find that a 2

CHAPTER 1. Why Should You Care About The Next Generation?

year old child can use a mobile phone and operate some other electrical gadgets that are located within their reach. Often they have found out how to use these gadgets without the aid of an instruction manual and guidance from someone older than them. You will also find that the average youth knows more about social media than their parents. When I was a youth, whenever I was away from my parents or my friends, my communication was largely done via postcards and coin boxes. Now, everyone has access to smart mobile phones, which gives us access to social media platforms at our finger tips. The ease of social media access has even influenced communications within families. We no longer have to talk. The modern day youth definitely has a lot more to worry about. The parents of modern day youths also have more to be concerned about. Wouldn't you agree with me that all these distraction can make it more difficult for youths to make decisions and stay focused? We must stand up and take more interest in the world that our children are growing up in, in order to support them, through their decision making.

As a youth pastor who has extended her ministry to communities and the world as a youth coach, I believe that God has entrusted me to meet the needs of the youth with love and humility on behalf of Christ. I strongly believe that other adults holding positions such as parents, carers, youth workers/leaders, teachers and community leaders, you have all been put in the place of trust and authority. You are trusted to be good role models for the next generation. The next generation are looking up to you for good advice, guidance and direction. What you sow into the next generation is what you will receive back from them. Not only have you and I been put in the position of trust and authority, we will also be held accountable for what we sow into the life of the next generation.

Whilst children are developing into young adults I believe they are faced with similar challenges that you and I faced as we were growing up. The lessons you have learned can help to shape the physical, emotional, mental, vocational, social and financial needs of developing youth today.

If you really want a future that produces a better for your future generation, than the results you have achieved out of life so far, then you need to do something about it. And don't say it can't be better than this because there is always room for improvement.

The next generation are our future. They are the ones that we will leave behind. So I ask this question. What generation do you want to raise? And to the youth - What generation do you want to be?

Chapter 2
Youth and the Evolution

CHAPTER 2
Youth and the Evolution

> *"I see no hope for the future of our people if they are dependent on the frivolous youth of today. For certainly, all youths are reckless beyond words. When I was a boy we were taught to be discreet and respectful of our elders, but the present youths are exceedingly wild and impatient."* **Hesiod (Exact date not known).**

Can you believe that Hesiod's quote above was made in 8th century BC? If this statement was made so long ago, then would it be fair to say that youths haven't changed? And if youths haven't changed, then what is it about today's youths that's causing all the attention? What follows is known to me and in other scholars that have taken an interest in the study of how youths have evolved.

The Youth Evolution

The Youth Evolution is the transition that young people have passed through, over the years. It is how the culture or behaviour of youths has evolved over a period of time. This takes into consideration, the cause of the evolution. Have you ever said the phrase, *'back in my days'* or *"when I was your age"*? Aren't these phrases that you grew up to hear your parents and other adults say to you? I know my parents used to say it to me and now I often say the same thing to my children and other social conversations. Isn't strange that some of the things we, as adults, say now is just what our parents used to say to us?

Even though there seems to be a pattern in the language used over generations, the changes that each generation has experienced are varied. This variation may be the cause of the same language being used through varying generations. Especially as each generation have been faced with different challenges which may not have been well managed by the previous generations.

The Youth Evolution

The information below is based on the generations from the western countries.

Generation X
Born: 1966 - 1976
Youthful Period: 1979 - 2001 *(Age rage 13 - 25)*
Age in 2015: 39 - 49

I happen to fall into this generation and on average, this generation tends to be the parents of the generation Z which are currently our next generation.

Studies show that youths of generation X were exposed to fashion trends, music and media. They tended to pick and act upon the slangs they are obtained from music videos and TV programme's. Radio stations were also very much in form. Family life was still a close unit with a majority still highly dependent on their parents, however the rates of divorce increased amongst their parents, which started a new emotional trend within the lives of youths.

As for me, the best form of communication available during my youth was a BT land line, BT coin box and cellular phone which was only available to the rich and mighty. I can still remember the big IBM computers and the black and white screen. I also still remember when I saw my first cellular phone. It must have been around 1990. I was so excited, but thought it was definitely too big for me to even desire to have one of my own. The price was also way out of my range.

Transportation was available till late hours in some parts of the world, such as in London, and most youths were heavily reliant on public transport as their mode of transport.

This generation were already exposed to the use of drugs such as cannabis and LSD.

As we approached the millennium, this seems to have changed drastically. I mean, I had a mobile phone that I purchased at £300. I had passed my driving test and had my own car. I was sharing a two-bedroom flat with my cousin and all of this as an undergrad who was fast approaching graduation. This was not the case with just me, but for most of my peer group. I can say that the trend of being dependant on your parents had started to decline with this generation.

Generation Y

Born: 1977 - 1994
Youthful Period: 1990 - 2019 *(Age rage 13 - 25)*
Age in 2015: 21 - 38

The generation in this category grew up (or should I say are still growing up) in a world that is ever-changing especially within the area of mass communication and the internet. The introduction of Face book in 2004 was welcomed positively and adapted to with ease by generation Y.

Generation Y are sophisticated and technology savvy as most of them have been introduced to it during their youth. Due to the de-monopolisation of services such as telephone and TV, there was an increase in these services which birthed rapid expansions in TV channels, satellite radio, the internet, and telecommunications companies including mobile phones.

Patience started to run out with this generation as we moved to the fast passed world, where everything has to be ready in minutes and sometimes even seconds.

The rate of divorce is on the increase, exposing those in generation Y to a sense of brokenness and maybe more independence and reliance on their peer groups.

Access to public transportation is better and more frequent in a majority of large cities in the world. There is also an increase in the amount of young drivers as the price of cars and credit for purchase becomes easier for all.

Harmful drugs are now more readily available in society and usage in this group is on the increase. Generation Y are more likely to take up part-time jobs during the school holidays as opposed to studying. The argument is education is challenging and the employment world following graduation is challenging.

Generation Z
Born: 1995 - 2012
Youthful Period: 2008 - 2037 *(Age rage 13 - 25)*
Age in 2015: 3 - 20

This generation is also known as the iGeneration. The eldest in this generation will be 20years this year. As social and technological changes have been evolving for more than 20 years, it can be expected that this generation will grow up with high technological advances in media and their use of computers will be more internet-based.

This is the next generation that this book has set out to raise awareness about, even though some of these youths are currently captured as generation Y as well.

The iGeneration have grown up with the most sophisticated types of technology. Almost every youth I know currently have access to a mobile phone. I'm not talking about ordinary phones either. They have to be smart phones, which gives them on-the-move access to technology and the world of social media. Some youths are also fortunate enough to have access to their own personal tablets, the iPad, the laptops and now the smart watch. In addition to this, there seems to be an increase in the amount of youths that have their own TV, DVD players etc… in their rooms.

Degree choices are a lot wider than what was previously available to the previous generations. More of this generation are likely to rely on their peers, the media and the internet for answers to their questions as the family unit becomes more disengaged.

I was watching the news recently and they were discussing how not a lot of families have time to sit and dine together anymore. Not only that, dinner is now normally in front of the TV whilst watching a programme. No more family discussions.

The iGeneration are presented with the opportunity, or should I say, the challenge of growing up in a world where their options are without limits. The question I ask is, will they be able to handle this challenge / opportunity well enough to impact their lives in a positive way.

I was at a public speakers' event recently, when I was presented with the opportunity to have a conversation with a grandfather who is from the baby boom generation (the generation before generation X). He was telling me how his 3-year-old grandchild had picked up an iPhone and operated it easily at the age of 1. His grandchild had picked up on how to use the phone simply by watching his parents using it. The child was never taught. This is the generation that are following the iGeneration and studies have not even begun on them yet.

The iGeneration is definitely fast paced and we need to keep up with them in order to coach and guide them in the usage of the information available today, in order to ensure they are making the right decision relating to their future.

A majority of the present day family is made up of parents from Generation X and Baby Boom who may have lost track of the current affairs that can impact their iGeneration children. Even teachers and some community leaders fall into the same category as their parents. Who is actually keeping up with the changes, and who is guiding Generation Z?

Some generations of parents repeat the way they were raised by their parents (good or bad), some end up doing it the opposite to the way they were raised and others just recreate the rules based on their life experience. However, how many parents are doing it in line with the challenges presented by the evolution?

Would it then be fair to assume that the lack of support available to the iGeneration is a contributing factor to the statistics below?

- 1 in 5 children grow up in workless households (higher than any EU country)
- 1 in 11, 16-18 year olds are not in education, training or employment
- High teenage pregnancies
- High rate of 15/16 year-old drug users
- 1 in 6, 16-24 year olds are victims of violence

The above stats were obtained from The Coaching Academy training materials 2015.

Youth Ministry Evolution

The youth evolution has also had an impact on the evolution of the youth ministry.

I remember when I was very young (I'm a generation X), I can only remember having the children's church and the adult church. My understanding, was that once you were between 16-18, you were considered old enough to part take out of the adult church. It was a great privilege to say to Sunday school teachers that you were no longer a member of their class. It was pride to be a member of the adult church and getting involved in different activities. Back then most families attended the same church and worshiped in the same faith.

However by the late 1990's, the same church initiated a youth ministry for the first time. The idea behind that was to empower the youths so that they would have a say in the running and development of the church. All in the mission of retention. The church had taken note that some younger members of the church where leaving the church for new and dynamic churches, so they thought if they empowered youths in our church then they are more likely to stay with the church. The only problem was the dynamism that the youths had to offer was considered to be "outrageous" by the adult church. The youths were taking the church outside its comfort zone and the leaders didn't like it. The adult population couldn't handle it. The youth ministry within the church didn't last as the opposition was stronger than them. The retention plan failed and a lot of youths ended up leaving the church.

What you'll find in most churches now is that they will have a children's church, a teenage church and a youth ministry catering for young adults. This presents them the opportunity to run church services as they wish.

However, even the creation of the singular youth church still didn't solve the problem, because now you will find that many youths do leave the church where it was once considered "the family church". Some will end up in other worship centres that are in most cases different to the worship centres that their family goes to or used to attend. Unfortunately, some just end up giving up on the faith. Now, it is no longer uncommon to have families worshiping at different centres, even congregations. Some families are even worshiping in different faiths. This is because the concept of the evolution is also having an impact on people's way of thinking and reasoning.

It's not just the structure of the church, or family worship that has changed. The topics for discussions are now broader than the Bible. For example, in our youth church you will find that our teaching is centred around topics such as Sex, Drugs, Peer pressure, other religions, fashion and even the world of social media. Would you agree with me that the topics (as a Generation X) are ones that were never discussed whilst we were growing up? The need to bring these topics into the church environment is because they are topics that seem to be dominating the information world nowadays. These topics appear to be growing concerns for developing youths, and if they are not addressed in the home, in the ministry or in the community, then we lose or at the very minimum reduce their chance for success.

The service, the songs and the teaching for the next generation has changed. The world is now presented with different pastors who have different teachings especially when the denomination of worship centres are different from each other. The most important thing for the youth ministry is to ensure that members are focused on their spiritual development but also factoring the concept of modern day challenges.

Every generation has experienced a time of great change. Generation Z are being raised during a period of rapid changes. If you take the time to understand the movement in the world of Generation Z, then you can begin to understand their current and future challenges. This will, in return, present you with a better choice of strategy on how to adopt to meet the needs of the iGeneration.

Chapter 3

Youth Influencers

CHAPTER 3
Youth Influencers

As a youth develops through the transition phases, they develop their self-concept which is influenced by several variables. These can include, but are not limited to, family members, mentors, peers, role models, lifestyle and culture. During the development of their self-concept they are challenged with making choices that will affect their present and future outcomes.

Below, I discuss some of the main influencers that I, my children and the youths that I have had the opportunity to work with, have experienced.

Parents & The Family Circle

In my family, I am child number three and number ten. You may be wondering how that is possible. Let me explain. You see, between my biological mum and my dad I am number three. However, to just my dad I was child number ten. Yes, you may have guessed, I was born into an African polygamous family. My dad was blessed with three wives and 17 children (well he thought it was a blessing). Fortunately, he was wealthy enough to build a house for each of his wives. I grew up living with my mum, as did my other siblings. However, during the holidays, my father would make sure that we all went to visit each mother's house and then spend some time with him. All of us together, meaning with daddy and mummy Ikeja (Dad's first wife) and the children that were old enough to look after themselves. During the time we spent with him, the most valuable time we would get with him would be 5a.m. every morning during family prayers. He used this time as his training time with us, I guess, as he didn't have any other time in the day to spend with us. He was a very busy man running multi-million dollar (international currency) companies and travelling a lot. In addition to that, he was well sought after by members of the community and the church.

CHAPTER 3. Youth Influencers

Growing up in a polygamous family at the time wasn't unusual, as most Nigerian families were of a polygamous circle. However, the approach that fathers, who were considered the head of the family, took to manage this very complicated family unit landed different results. Considering that my father had three wives and 17 children, he appeared to have managed his home well.

I must have been about age 9 when I came to the realization that I was number three and ten in my family. This happened during a conversation I was having with my best friend, Stephanie, at boarding school. The conversation went like this.

Stephanie: "So how many children do your parents have?"

Yetunde: "Well let me see", I replied as I started to count my fingers and calling out my siblings' names. At that time we were 12 from my dad and 4 from my mum and dad. As I started to respond to Stephanie's question, it began to dawn on me that my ranking in the family (no matter which way you looked at it) was quite low. That one question had led to so many other thoughts which influenced a lot of my decisions about my future.

Boarding school was full of young people with different backgrounds. Some were from one parent families, where one parent had passed away or had left the family. Others were fortunate enough to have both parents together and alive. Very few had adopted parents. It was at boarding school that I developed my knowledge of divorce and other types of families. It took me quite some time to get used to these different types of family unit, just like I guess it took my friend's then time to understand my family unit as this is not common or acceptable in the UK.

With the varied family types that existed in the boarding school, you can imagine what we the children were like. Some of us preferred to be at boarding school just because it meant we were escaping family issues at home. The behavioural characters of some of us demonstrated that home life was not quite the way it should have been.

The family environment that I grew up in and the ones that I discovered at boarding school influenced me to arrive at the conclusion that I was never going to get married. I wanted children though and I think I spent most of my child hood trying to figure out how I was going to have children without getting married. The process I was taught was that you study as far as possible, graduate, get a job, get married and have children. You may be wondering why I didn't want to get married. I believed that the chance of me ending up with either a polygamist or a divorcee was quite high. Why was it high? At my young tender age, most of my friends and close relatives were in one of these family situations. My experience of growing up in a polygamous family taught me that it is not a healthy type of family life style that people should be living. There was always trouble, confusion, competition and unfair treatment. It was a situation that I couldn't wait to get out of and most certainly not one I wished to get myself involved with for the rest of my life.

Even though at a younger age, I thought I never wanted to get married I am now married today and we are blessed with children. How I overcame my mind-set about marriage, the family unit and my belief is definitely a story for another book.

Knowing that I am number three and number ten, I knew I had to work hard to be a survivor. I became self-sufficient as soon as age permitted me to. I never depended on my dad and mum unless it was something they wanted me to do and it was beyond my financial capabilities. I came to the conclusion that being independent was the only way I could protect myself from the challenges presented by being a member of a polygamous family unit.

Parents are a critical source of influencers to the developing youth. From a very young age (younger than you may wish to imagine), they pick up on our actions and form their own beliefs from there. It's the lack of appropriate communications that presents challenges which may weaken the influence you have on your child.

Peers & Friends

Due to the sometimes lack of appropriate communications between youths, their parents or families, young people are more likely to talk to their peers as they will value their peers' opinions more than other influences. As a result, they are more likely to conform to peer pressure than the beliefs that have been communicated to them by their parents whilst growing up. Especially when these beliefs have not been deeply rooted in them.

I remember clearly when I joined the local college in North London. Coming from a private boarding school, you can imagine that I may have had challenges fitting to the college. The students, teachers and culture were completely different to what I had been brought up with in boarding school.

College started to feel very uncomfortable as I had no friends. I remember that I used to go home for lunch instead of staying with my peers.

Gradually, I started to mix with a group of girls who appeared to be sensible, but in order to fit into the group, my fashion began to change, my English accent changed, my hair style changed and my attitude changed. The new me was more like someone who was raised by a Jamaican family as opposed to a Nigerian family who was studied at a private boarding school.

One day, I found myself attending the Oasis night club in Hackney, East London. That experience was definitely the most uncomfortable experience of my life. I mean here's a girl (now an adult) who had been raised to be responsible, finding herself in this type of place. Thank God the night club was shut down by the police a couple of weeks after my first experience because someone had been shot dead during a club session. I thought to myself "That could have been me, if I had been there that night."That became the end of my clubbing life and a return to my studying life.

Comparing the peer pressure that I experienced then to the one that young people are faced with today, it seems like very minor stuff. You hear about all sorts of groups through the media nowadays. Groups like gangsters that deal in drugs, bullying, stealing, killings and prostitution. The thing is, young people will go with who seems to be giving them the love and attention they need and desire. This is more likely to be from their peers, if nothing is coming from their families.

Young people that come from a fairly decent home are also caught up in the motion of peer pressure, which has been made easier with the development of technology.

It is not such a problem for young people to turn around to their peers for support, so long as the peers they are turning to will have a positive impact on them and not a negative impact. It is worth noting that a positive peer group cannot be guaranteed.

It is therefore important that you, as parents, know your children's friends very well so you can know who they are being influenced by.

Technology and modern day living

The McCridle Research Company 2015 reported that Gen Z are the first truly global generation, as discussed in the previous chapter. Even though music, movies and celebrities have been globally available to us in the previous generations, technology and globalisation have led to the circulation of up-to-date news relating to fashion, entertainment, social trends and the like to be even more global.

Recent studies have shown that over half of children between the ages of nine and 17 have internet cable or satellite television in their bedrooms. Leaving the kids to own devices and they can choose what they want to watch on their own. With the introduction of smart phones and devices such as the tablet they don't even need to be in their bedrooms before they can have access to TV and the internet.

I was shocked to find what the results of the Taylor Thomas (April, 2011) statistics states. These are as follows:

- 93% of teens ages 12-17 go online
- 69% of teens have their own computer
- 63% of teens use their phone to get online
- 24% of teens with a console use it to go online

A lot of teenagers have grown up with social media being a part of their world, and most cannot remember life without it.

Global and national friendships are now easier to form via the endless list of social media channels that are now available. Gen Y and Gen Z are well connected by their peers via social media. They can be easily influenced by this connection of the online community.

Under the "freedom of expression" rule, the government and the courts have given cable and internet suppliers the right to broadcast explicit sex, violence, nudity and profanity to your children and grandchildren. Unfortunately, this presents a danger to our community and our world. The danger of social media is that it gives child predators easier access to the next generation.

On a positive note, the internet can actually be made a safe place for young people to connect with others and certainly somewhere that I recommend for their daily development. However, certain areas of cyberspace are not appropriate for children due to the exposure they may have to certain activities that may not be suitable for children. For this reason, in 2009, the UK Council for Child Internet Safety (UKCCIS) developed the "click clever" and "click safe" code. These two codes are for child internet safety strategies, encouraging all children's organisations to teach on the code of "Zip it", "Block it", and "Flag it" whenever they find a case that warrants these actions as they surf the net. The purpose for the design of these codes are to:

- "Give parents the confidence to be able to help their children enjoy the internet safely.

- Help children and young people understand how their online experiences can expose them to risk." *Safeguarding in a digital world. CCPAS – Setting Standards in Safeguarding. 2011.*

The Zip It Code is to inform parents how to encourage their children to keep their private information safe and to watch what they say on the internet. Private information is classified as below:

- Full name
- Photos
- Postal or email addresses
- School information
- Mobile or home contact numbers
- Details of places they like to spend time

Under this code, parents, youth teachers and leaders are also encouraged to teach the youth that they are not to meet with someone they have met online no matter if they have known them in the online world for a long time or not.

Children's private information can also be kept safe online by having privacy settings on all your technical devices, i.e. computers, laptops and iPad etc...

Another tip under this code is that children should be encouraged to use nicknames for chat rooms and instant messaging services. This will prevent people from accessing the child's account and protects their identity.

Passwords are to be kept secret and changed on a regular basis.

Block it Code

This code encourages children to:

- Block anyone that sends offensive messages
- Children are not to open unknown links and attachments
- Delete suspicious emails or attachments

"One of the main ways children can come across inappropriate content online is through search results. Most search engines include a "safe search" option that excludes results containing inappropriate images or keywords.

Parents and organisations can also install parental control software to filter out harmful and inappropriate content for computers and some mobile phones and games consoles." *Safeguarding in a digital world. CCPAS – Setting Standards in Safeguarding. 2011*

Flag it Code

This code simply exists in order to encourage children to report their online concerns to parents or a trusted adult.

You should inform your children to notify you if a "friend" of theirs from the social media forum encourages them to meet them somewhere, as this may lead to an event outside their control or yours.

If a child does experience inappropriate content online, report it to the website it appears on and contact your local police.

As a sheep needs a shepherd, in the same manor your children need you to be a loving and observant parent. You cannot afford to be ignorant about technology. You need to know. You need to keep up so that you can provide the right guidance for their safety and future success.

Teachers & Lecturers

As teachers and lecturers within educational institutes, community groups or religious institutions, you need to understand that what you say and do to the children that are in your care can have a negative or positive impact on them not only during class period or the period of time they spend with you. The way you communicate with them can impact them for the rest of their life.

On the other hand, the expectation laid upon teachers & lecturers nowadays are very high especially in the academic arena. Further to conversations with parents and the members of other local communities, the general expectations for teachers and lecturers ranged from acting as counsellors, motivators, behavioural experts and sometimes mentors. More so than never before, some teachers are expected to take responsibility for something that parents should be taking responsibility for.

A research that was carried out by The Coaching Academy in 2007-2008, which involved participation from 50 school teachers across the country showed the following:

> *"Teachers are expected to be social workers, counsellors, welfare workers, motivators, coaches, time management experts, behaviour therapist, able to plan and deliver inspirational lessons that meet the individual personal learning needs of 30+ children; as well as be creative with their thinking, prepare for meetings, mark work, pass Ofsted inspections, be part of extra curriculum activities, hold parents evenings, write reports, discipline bad behaviour, deal with abuse and extreme behaviour, be inclusive, put up with unrealistic expectations, have no personal life or work life balance and now, as one teacher recently told me, include skills for life which means five cultural experiences a week for the children! And on top of that, teach them something that enables them to pass examinations."*

CHAPTER 3. Youth Influencers

With all the above emotions from a community of teachers, it can often be expected that teachers will feel challenged in their roles. If the challenges presented to them are over-stretching them, this can lead to them feeling depressed, overwhelmed, anxious, frustrated, angry and confused.

The purpose of teachers is for them to educate their students or members whilst supporting and inspiring them to achieve the best that they can. However, the expectations laid upon them and the different characteristics of children that now attend their institutions may sometimes challenge teachers with having the motivation that they need to do their job well. This can sometimes lead to students being treated unfairly. This may lead to the teacher communicating with students by negative talk. Unfortunately, this may also lead to peers doing their own negative talk to that same child, which will not help the devolving youth. At this stage, the only option for this child may be negative behaviour. You will also find that not all teachers have the best answers to everything. Their advice and teaching will only go as far as what they know.

There was a young lady that I had coached because she was not achieving her expected results and her teachers were under-grading her even though they knew she could achieve more than the set target grade. The teacher's explanation was they didn't want to set her hopes too high. Through her coaching sessions, she had mentioned to me that she didn't believe she could achieve the A grades that her tutors said that she could achieve. I asked her why she had this belief. For a while, she couldn't understand why she had this belief, until one day she said "I know where all of my unbelief came from". She came to the realisation that her negative thoughts came from her experience at primary school.

Through the coaching session, I discovered that whenever she wanted to do something in school, she would be told by teachers that she couldn't do that. To make matters worse, she had friends that always got picked to do the things she wanted to get involved with instead of her. She had carried this belief with her for about 6 years prior to receiving coaching from me.

Once she was able to identify the root of the problem, she was able to say to herself that she was now in a different school and environment. As the teachers and her new friends believed in her, she only needed to believe in herself and prove negative talkers wrong.

By gaining the confidence in herself through her own self-belief, she managed to break the thoughts of under-achieving and she is now a very high achiever.

On a different occasion, there was a time when we had a youth come and visit our church and they asked "Why is there so much judgment in the church?" Feeling shocked at the question but trying to compose my response at the same time, "Judgment in the church! What do you mean by that?" I replied. "Well, you see when people in church see my tattoo they look and speak to me in a funny way. It really makes me uncomfortable. I think they have an issue with my tattoo, and I know that the Bible says that we should not judge. So why are they judging me?"he replied.

Even though the discussion went on for much longer and I tried to get this young man to find a way to approach the reaction of others to him, it was quite clear that the damage had already been done. He seemed to have been experiencing the same thing at every place of worship that he had gone to.

As leaders, in any capacity you need to be conscious of your negative talking, especially when you are interacting with the iGeneration as they are more sensitive and are less likely to ask for explanations and so they are quick to draw conclusions that may have a negative impact on their entire life.

CHAPTER 3. Youth Influencers

The Law

You may be aware that young people have certain rights in some shape or form. A label given to young people's rights is "rights without responsibility."

You may not know that there is an international agreement that outlines the rights of a child. This is known as the United Nations Convention on the Rights of a Child (UNCRC), and has been put in place to protect the rights of children so that their rights will not be overlooked.

"The Convention States that young people have three main rights, which must be considered in all interventions involving young people:

- Non-Discrimination - (refers to article 2)
- Best Interest - (refers to article 3)
- The Child's view - (refers to article 12)

Other rights the convention gives to children are with respect to civil and political rights. These are to do with children but to take part in Society, and to be involved in matters which are important to them.

It's amazing how the children know the law and how some have used the law to their advantage in some situations. The law governing them and the rights they are entitled to surprisingly is taught to them at school, and in a lot of cases, parents don't know the law that the UN or the government governs their children with.

Some decisions that children, especially young adults, make can be influenced by the law, especially in countries that the law is well-publicized and taught in schools.

Chapter 4
Your Children, Your Future

CHAPTER 4
Your Children, Your Future

"Greatest Love Of All" - By Whitney Houston

I believe the children are our future
Teach them well and let them lead the way
Show them all the beauty they possess inside
Give them a sense of pride to make it easier
Let the children's laughter remind us how we used to be

Everybody's searching for a hero
People need someone to look up to
I never found anyone who fulfilled my needs
A lonely place to be
And so I learned to depend on me
[Chorus:]
I decided long ago, never to walk in anyone's shadows
If I fail, if I succeed
At least I'll live as I believe
No matter what they take from me
They can't take away my dignity
Because the greatest love of all
Is happening to me
I found the greatest love of all
Inside of me
The greatest love of all
Is easy to achieve
Learning to love yourself
It is the greatest love of all

CHAPTER 4. Your Children, Your Future

> I believe the children are our future
> Teach them well and let them lead the way
> Show them all the beauty they possess inside
> Give them a sense of pride to make it easier
> Let the children's laughter remind us how we used to be
> *[Chorus]*
> And if, by chance, that special place
> That you've been dreaming of
> Leads you to a lonely place
> Find your strength in love

Like me, some were born with a silver spoon in their mouth, surrounded by riches, a roof over their head with access to the best education and facilities in the world. Growing up in a very strict Christian home alongside all of the above, the expectation is surely, nothing could possibly go wrong. Yes it sure can.

I remember when I was growing up, I used to desire to provide my children with the same opportunity as the one my parents gave me. You know the good home, the good boarding school education and the rest. My parents had made it all look so simple; I thought that I could do it too. However, that was far from reality. I often ask myself, why is this so? The answer didn't hit me till recently. The conclusion I came to was that I was never taught the survival trade. I had a good education and I was raised well in order to get a decent job. Life has taught me that it's a little more than getting a degree and a decent job that can get you the type of wealth that I desired to have. So many opportunities have been missed because of the focus on a decent job.

So now, looking back seeing what my parents achieved, all are barely standing. I believe they did their best as far as they understood it. I did graduate and get a decent job immediately after graduation. Unfortunately, the job that all those years of education prepared me for hasn't satisfied me financially, spiritually or emotionally. I have therefore come to the conclusion that there was a lot missing in my upbringing. Or was what my parents did enough for their time? Times have changed and times are still changing. Parents need to take a more interested and proactive approach to their children's future success. It's no longer about raising children. It's about raising successful children.

I do believe that children are our future, and if we teach them well, then they will lead the way. Your children are your next generation. The ideal situation is that your children will be greater than you and that they will achieve more than the generations before them are achieving or would have achieved, by the time they pass on the baton to them.

You may believe that once a child has gone to school, then they have been taught. Perhaps you believe (as I used to) that after biblical and academic education, then that's all a child needs. The fast track education about the next generation I have been exposed to over recent years has left me to be convinced beyond reasonable doubt that it is more than that. The saying goes; wisdom is the application of knowledge and understanding. In other words, if you are educated and you do not apply the level of education attained to your way of delivery, then you do not have wisdom.

There are four aspects to human nature. These are known as the Physical, Social/Emotional, Spiritual and Mental Abilities. You, as a parent or an adult in the position of responsibility for developing children, should focus on shaping the life of this young child in all areas of their human nature. By helping youths to develop steadily and effectively in these areas means that you may have given them the guidance and power that would enable them to use their wisdom to create their security.

Your next generation must be taught to honour people in authority and to give respect to them. Don't just teach them the educational route alone. Don't teach them the spiritual route alone. Teach them every aspect of life because it all counts towards building them a successful future. What has life taught you? What is the government doing and how is it going to impact your children and their future? Pay attention to these questions and teach your children your concluding answers. Better still, let them conclude the right answer for themselves.

It is by them knowing truly that they believe in themselves and they desire for great things for themselves.

The song at the beginning of this chapter was released by Whitney Houston in 1986, when I believe I must have been a teenager. I remember it was one of my favourite songs at the time. I used to meditate on the words at any given opportunity, and even now as a mother of teenagers I still meditate on the lyrics.

"Show them all the beauty they possess inside."

Survival in reality is about the beauty that you possess inside of you. Your internal thoughts, beliefs and values are what makes you or breaks you. If you can demonstrate to your children that they are valuable and they are beautiful inside, then they will have confidence to achieve what they want to achieve.

A high percentage of the youths that I have had the opportunity to work with, do lack self-confidence. This lack of self-confidence has mainly been derived from negative talk from their parents and influencers that they are exposed to. If you don't believe in your children, then who will believe in them?

When I'm doing mentoring or coaching sessions, I can sometimes feel and see that some of these children are feeling lost inside. Some of the youths that I've worked with have often told me things like "nobody cares" and "what's the point?" Some parents, because they have split up or got lost in their own world, have left their children to themselves probably thinking the other parent should be picking things up and between them, nobody is picking anything up.

I know the challenges of being a parent and in the past I've often failed to show my children the beauty they possess inside, but through the desire that I had to be a better parent, youth pastor and coach, I knew my strategy had to change. I first had to listen, understand and then figure out how best to implement the changes that I needed to make.

"Give them a sense of pride to make it easier."

It was during a coaching session that I had, that made me realise the power of the sense of pride. During this particular session, the group was asked how many times we celebrated our children when they did something well. Quite a few of us said that we do celebrate our children, but what came to light for me was I would say well done and immediately, I would say something like "but you know you could have done better than that." or say for example in one of my children came 3rd, I would say "what happened to 1st place?" Coaching taught me the impact that this kind of response can have on a child. The impact is not a positive one as it can de-motivate your child not only for the short term, but for a life time.

I used to attend my youngest son's football practises. I was there physically but my mind wasn't on the game. What I was doing was to use his practice session to catch up on my phone calls, reading or writing. It was during one of my coaching sessions that I decided to stop taking my phone and other things that would distract my attention from my son's football practice, so that I can actually watch him play. Prior to this time, my son had often asked me why I sometimes don't watch him whilst he is playing football. I didn't know he noticed. You see, if he played well, I didn't celebrate him like the other parents would celebrate their children, because I wasn't watching the game. Obviously, this didn't give him a sense of pride, if anything, it made him feel as though I didn't care about his talent. That coaching session helped me to realise that I had to change for the sake of my son.

CHAPTER 4. Your Children, Your Future

Everybody's searching for a hero, people need someone to look up to.

One of my coachee's once said to me that they had no one to look up to because no one really cared about them. This particular person's parents were divorced and the youth's time was split between his parents. The youth felt that neither of his parents presented characteristics that they could say inspired them to become like them.

With all the choice and distraction that is available today, it should only be right that parents should be the ones that their children are looking up to.

Who is your next generation looking up to? Are you a good enough example?

Teach them to love themselves.

The centre of success is love and happiness. If you cannot love your children, then they cannot experience love and may possibly never learn to love themselves. When you love yourself, then it is easier to love other people.

The first time I really heard about loving myself was about 3 years ago. Prior to that, I don't think I really loved myself, because I didn't know it was a requirement. Or did I think it was vain to love myself? Even though I had read in the bible several time before "love your neighbour as yourself." Mark 12:31 New International Version. This only sank in a couple of years ago during my personal development on the Esther's mentoring programme run by RCCG Jesus House, UK. In discovering self-love, I came to the realisation that I was punishing myself for past mistakes and I hated myself for it. I had to learn how to forgive myself for my past mistakes and let them go. I then gave myself permission to love myself. It wasn't an overnight process, but earlier on this year I overcame my challenges through professional and personal coaching. I can honestly say that loving myself has made the world of difference in my marriage, ministry, work and my relationship with my children. I am now showing my children and other children that I have the opportunity to work with, how to love themselves.

I remember once, when there was a discussion at our youth church about parents needing to go out to work for money in order to provide for their families, which meant that they couldn't be there all the time. One of the members raised her hand and said "It's not about money all the time". "Yeah, you're right". I responded following a short pause. I termed this young lady's response to mean so many things. One, that you can't buy a child's true love. Two, you need to set some quality time with your children. Three, you need to listen to what they are saying and meet them at their point of need.

I want you to take a moment and to think about the below quote from mother Teresa, and then write down what it means to you.

> "If you want world peace, go home and love your family." **Mother Teresa**

"I never found anyone who could fill my needs, a lonely place to be and so I learned to depend on me."

When young people cannot find anyone to fill their needs, they become dependent on themselves. This doesn't always work out to be the best solution for the children as they may not be mentally matured or experienced enough to depend on themselves. This may lead to making wrong decisions about themselves and their futures.

Every developing young person needs support in filling their needs and parents are a child's most powerful role model. In the absence of parents, then teachers, family members and other leaders have a sense of duty in supporting young people to filling their needs.

TNCG runs regular group parental coaching sessions that supports parents in developing their parental skills in order to improve themselves and their children. You can register for a session by visiting www.TheNextChosenGeneration.com.

Generation Wipe Out

There's a story about a man called Eli in the Bible. Eli was a High Priest in the line of Ithamar. He was also Judge of Israel at Shiloh for 40 years. Although he was the High Priest, Eli did not have a focus for the future of his children, who should have been his successors. He failed to discipline the behaviour of his sons, Hophni and Phinehas. His sons took sacrificial meat from the altar for them to eat; they committed adultery with women in the sanctuary. Eli was aware of what his sons were doing, but he failed to discipline, correct or teach them that what they were doing was wrong. God had told Samuel that Eli's family would be punished for blaspheming against God. Samuel told Eli about this and Eli said that the Lord should do what He thinks is best under the circumstances. Later, as they accompanied the Ark against the Philistines, Eli's sons were killed. When Eli was informed of the death of his sons, he fell backwards while seated in a chair, broke his neck and died. Even though Eli's linage continued up until the time of Solomon, eventually Eli's lineage was brought to an end. *This story is narrated in line with 1 Samuel 2.*

Eli failed to do the right thing regarding his sons. Many times when I've read this Bible passage, I've always asked myself, where was their mother? Where were the members of the community? Could no one help Hophni and Phinehas? Had they been allowed to progress with their bad behaviour for so long that they became uncontrollable or gone beyond the state of help? The story does however demonstrate that God held Eli ultimately accountable for the behaviour of his sons, because he was the only person that God gave the warning about his sons to.

If you do not care about the future and the success of the next generation especially with the challenges presented to you in the current evolution, you run the risk of wiping the next generation out. Not just your generation but the generation of communities and in the world on a larger scale.

The bible states that

> *"Behold, children are a heritage from the Lord, The fruit of the womb is a reward. Like arrows in the hand of a warrior, so are the children of one's youth. Happy is the man who has quiver full of them; They shall not be ashamed, But shall speak with their enemies in the gate."* **Psalm 127:3-5, New King James Version**

This means that children are valuable assets to their parents. As a parent you need to know that your children are a valuable asset to you and your generations to come.

As teachers, community workers and leaders, you need to know that children are assets to our world. The child you are teaching now has a future. You don't know what the future holds for them. You have the power now to make a positive or a negative impact in that child's life now. What impact will you make?

You are to care for the next generation and nurture them until they are grown and developed enough to live life as sensible adults.

Chapter 5

The New Approach for Focusing Youths for Success

CHAPTER 5
The New Approach for Focusing Youths for Success

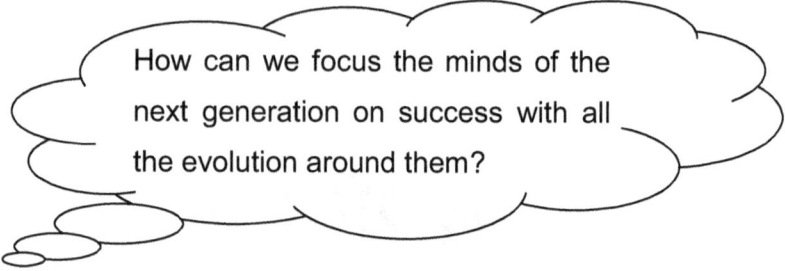

How can we focus the minds of the next generation on success with all the evolution around them?

In order to focus the minds of the iGeneration, you will need to get them engaged in what they are most passionate about. We no longer live in the age where children are living the dreams of their parents. The iGeneration have free minds and they are logical thinkers. You will need to discover their passion, know what is available to them in line with their passion and work with them in order to ensure they achieve their full potentials and their dreams. Coaching presents a platform that supports this transitional decision-making process.

Coaching is the result of a gentle evolution over several years that have grown due to the rate of demand for it. Coaching presents people with the opportunity to talk through the issues, feelings and challenges that they are experiencing without being judged or being told what to do. Coaching also helps you to identify their goals and gives them the support of an expert to support them through the journey to identify their desired goals.

Coaching is a conversation that takes place between the coach and their audience. If the session is one-to-one, then the conversation will be between the coach and the client. During the dialogue the coach will encourage and support the client as they progress to become the best they can be.

CHAPTER 5. The New Approach to Focusing Youths for Success

Coaching young people is intended to provide support for them in a positive and productive way. It provides youths with the opportunity to support them in order for them to make clear choices and decisions about their future.

The core skills that coaching presents are:

Questioning: to explore what goal, problem or challenge they are faced with.

Listening to understand

Time and **Space** for the individual to think

Presents them with an **Opportunity** for **Options** to be explored

Allows choices to be selected

The challenges that young people are presented with nowadays coupled with the decisions they need to make, gives the coaching process the upper hand in supporting young people through their decision-making process at crucial transition periods.

It is apparent through the previous chapters that some young people will not be presented with so many choices, as their parents may have made all their life decisions for them before they were even born. So these children grow up, doing what their parents have raised them to become. However, during their adult life, they may become overwhelmed at the thought that what they are doing is the wrong thing, as they would have been living their life for someone else. The years of hard work and all the funding that went towards getting them to where they are or who you want them to be has now been wasted.

Would you agree with me, that if you had the platform that gave you the assurance that you knew what you were doing was right and you had the right professional support to help you in reaching your goals that perhaps you would have made a better success of life. Coaching presents a platform for making clear decisions under this circumstance.

The coaching tools that I use to support young people to focus on themselves and their future, enables them to be realistic, take responsibility for their choices, anticipate obstacles and explore proper planning. For more information about the coaching I offer, please visit: www.TheNextChosenGeneration.com.

The New Approach – Case Study

A short while ago, I coached a teenager because of the challenges he was having at home. As he grew up, his parents began to give him more responsibilities in the house. To him he felt they no longer loved him and that they loved his younger brother more than him. As a result, he became rebellious because growing older to him meant that he could do what he liked when he liked. He also felt that no matter what he does, he will not get approval. He knew the part of the law that was on his side and he was more than happy to be creative with it in order to get away from home.

As the coaching session progressed, he realised that I was on his side and he started to discuss the sadness, anger, frustration and disappointment that he felt about the way he was treated at home. It also became apparent that he was developing a belief that he would never be good enough. I quickly shifted his negative belief by discussing the qualities that he had which would make him good enough. We also discussed the good things he does for his family and the times when he has been obedient. By the end of the session, the young man walked out more positive about life than when he first started his coaching session.

The outcome of this session was that, that young man is now at peace with his family and the atmosphere at home has also improved.

CHAPTER 5. The New Approach to Focusing Youths for Success

Challenges for Youths.

There is always a lot of media coverage on the challenges that youths are experiencing. The news on a daily basis reports on one or more of the following relating to youths. Knife crime, binge drinking, assault, violence, drugs, peer pressure, mental health challenges, depression, physical, mental and sexual abuse, fitting in, having a social life and examination challenges.

These challenges are often linked to issues relating to their personal lives, i.e. being in one-parent families, alcohol and drug abuse families, parents or family members that are suffering from depression.

Even youths that have very supportive or affluent families are likely to experience negative behaviours, which maybe because of the high expectations set by their parents. This may also be caused by competition with their peers.

The Future of Coaching

Imagine your home or your school where the youths spend most of their time, and the environment is full of confident young people who engage more, making better relationship with teachers and parents. Their learning, knowledge and understanding develops. The youths are producing high quality work and are performing at their full potential. They are motivated to do well and succeed. Or possibly your home or learning environment is full of focused youths who know what they want in life and therefore are better behaved and they become improved in all aspects of their life.

Would you agree with me that this would make the life of teachers and parents a lot easier and a less stressful?

Youth coaching is now an internationally recognised effective method that provides young people with support and guidance to help them to cope with challenging situations as they develop into adulthood.

As technology continues to evolve, some young people are increasingly being exposed to cyber bullying, face-to-face bullying, peer pressure and other types of negative experiences through their social network. This often results in the victimised youth developing antisocial behaviours. The behaviour of young children and teenagers (whether good or bad) can impact the lives of their family members and can also extend to the community.

Coaching helps teens to discover themselves and gain the confidence in order to become who they were created to be.

Having a goal is an essential part of success. Without having a goal, you will not be focused and can therefore find yourself not achieving anything or losing track of your desired end result. A goal is a target to aim for, but in order to arrive at a goal, you need to know the options available to you. By young people setting goals for themselves, they will naturally become focused on this end goal and are less likely to want to do anything that will prevent them from achieving their goal. Coaching helps youths to identify realistic and achievable goals. For example, the Be–Do–Have coaching tool can be used to help youths to identify their life goals. The tool helps you to focus on what you want to BE, the DO element looks at what you want to do and they HAVE element looks at what you want have as a result of being who you want to be and doing what you want to do.

This tool is very effective because it allows youths to describe their dreams, desires, beliefs, passion and future goals with the right thinking concept, that are likely to generate a more realistic future that they can be motivated to focus on achieving.

CHAPTER 5. The New Approach to Focusing Youths for Success

Parental Coaching

During the period of the baby boomers, information was passed on during family gatherings such as prayer meetings and at dinner time when everybody sat round the table to dine together. The eldest or the head of the family would share the wisdom of life experiences for the younger generation to pass on.

Would you agree with me that more and more families are finding it difficult to keep up with this tradition? Here's the problem with this. The valuable time that you are missing out on means that valuable lessons are not being passed on, neither is there the time to focus on the behavioural patterns of your children. Unfortunately, these are lessons that school or university won't teach your children.

Parents are now faced with challenges that perhaps they have never experienced before. One of the most important realisations for parents is that being a parent is one of the most important jobs that you will do in life. With this in mind, you are also faced with the fact that you are in a lifelong relationship with your child and you want to do everything possible for your child, but the society that we now live in does not afford you the time to be there as much as you want or need to be, to listen and not judge, and to communicate effectively with your child.

There is high pressure on parents now, especially with youths getting a lot of media attention. The media is so focused on raising children issues that every time you read the papers, if they are not telling parents what children should and shouldn't eating, doing, watching and where to be hanging out, they are telling you about how social media and technology can take over their world.

Would you agree with me that being a parent can sometimes be overwhelming? The evolution has presented you with a world that makes your role as a parent challenging. Do you find that as a parent, you are screaming and shouting and you find it difficult to control your emotions at times? Or perhaps you have high expectations of your children and when they don't achieve your expectations, then you become judgemental about yourself and begin to feel that you are not good enough? As a result, you may now be taking your frustration out on your children.

Here's the thing, you cannot break your child's negative behaviour pattern that is presenting you with challenges in your present state. If anything, you will make it worse. Would you therefore agree with me that as your child's greatest influencer and most powerful role model, you would need to change in order for your child to change? Coaching can help you to boost your confidence and self-belief. Positive self-belief is important in the role of parenting, because whatever your beliefs are, are the beliefs that you are most likely to pass on to your next generation. The coaching process, especially when supported with the parent wheel tool can help to boost your confidence in becoming the parent you want to be.

Please take some time to complete the Parent Coaching Questionnaire below. See how you feel after completing it. If you would like to discuss your answers, please contact me at yetunde@yetundeadeshile.com.

Parent Coaching Questionnaire

"What three values are most important to you as a parent?

1.

2.

3.

What are your three most significant achievements as a parent?

1.

2.

3.

What is the greatest challenge that you have overcome as a parent?

What do you love most about being a parent?

What key skill makes you a good family problem-solver?

What would your child(ren) say is the best thing about having you as a parent?"

The Coaching Academy, 2015 - Diploma in Coaching within Education, Parent Coaching

Coaching in Youth Ministry

One of the challenges that youth ministries face is in having stability of the next generation in ministry. The evolution has exposed youths to a lot more via the internet, the use of social media platforms and mainly their peers. Youths are exposed to so much now with the increase of different faith establishments, this can sometimes lead them to be confused and because of limited engagement with the key family members, they may feel they have or are beginning to lose their identity.

There is now a real concern for youths in ministry because more and more are getting experiencing sexual abuse, pornography, emotional brokenness and technology seems to have re-written all the rules which has made matters worse.

Many youths are challenged by fear, lack of self-belief and the lack of love. Youths are faced with making the right decisions before someone else comes to make it for them.

Sometimes because their faith teaching hasn't been deeply rooted in them, they find it challenging to handle the problems that they are presented with. Often you will find that some believe that their parent's faith and service covers them for life. This obviously is not the case, as God deals with us as individuals.

The Bible in proverbs 22:6 says: *"Train up a child in the way he should go, And when he is old he will not depart from it."* The GROW coaching model presents a good platform to develop and keep youths focused on their future and their spiritual development. GROW stands for:

Goal setting – What is your spiritual goal?
Reality checking of the goal – Is this a realistic goal?
Options available – Who, what and how can you achieve this goal?
Will – How much/How important is it that you achieve this goal?

This model presents you in the youth ministry the opportunity to set yourself a faith-related goal that is realistic and achievable for you.

One thing to realise is that people in ministry are not exempt from the challenges of life. The Bible makes us understand that we will have trials and tribulations but it's the grace and the anointing from God that allows us to overcome our life challenges.

Coaching is a platform that will challenge youths in ministry and can help them to focus on their aspirations to develop their spirituality.

Chapter 6

Focus for Spiritual Success

CHAPTER 6
Focus for Spiritual Success

"Let no man despise thy youth; but be thou an example of the believers, in word, in conversation, in charity, in spirit, in faith, in purity". **1 Timothy 4:12**

The Bible here mentions that you should lead the next generation by example. In other words you are to practice what you preach. It is not good enough to say one thing and then do another thing in the presence of young people. This kind of behaviour only puts young people off, it distracts their attention and can potentially make them lose interest in the faith.

My experience of God is defined by the privilege of being born into a Christian family and being raised in the way of the Lord. Perhaps, though, you believe that God is of a different nature to you. You may still agree with me that it is important that you have something higher operating within you that provides you with divine strength when you need it. You need a Higher Power that you can open up to when you are at cross roads and need direction for the next step. You can only get this direction from your Higher Power if you have spiritual success.

As a Christian, my Higher Power is God and he is the one that I draw my strength from when I am weak. He gives me direction when I am lost and he guides me wherever I go.

As previously stated, your Higher Power may be drawn from a different belief but by following the steps below, you can achieve focus for spiritual success.

Five Fingers for Spiritual Success

If you want to develop your focus on achieving spiritual success, I recommend that you apply the Five Fingers for success as taught by Pastor EA Adeboye. Pastor EA Adeboye's Open Heaven,

2014 states the following as the five fingers for spiritual success: hearing, reading, studying, memorising and meditating:

❖ Hearing

- *"So then faith cometh by hearing, and hearing by the word of God."* **Romans 10:17**

    You need to hear words about and from your spiritual being. Not just words but teachings that you can apply to your life and situations in your life. Hearing is a very effective way to gain initial and foundational knowledge about the faith, especially when it's repetitive.

    As the knowledge and interest develops, the mind becomes more inquisitive about the faith.

❖ Reading

- *"And it shall be with him, and he shall read therein all the days of his life: that he may learn to fear the Lord his God, to keep all the words of this law and these statutes, to do them."***Deuteronomy 17:19**

    As a Christian, God's word is the source of your spiritual energy just as food is the source of your physical energy. You energise your spiritual energy by reading the Bible regularly. According to educationalists, regular reading helps you retain up to 25% of what we have read.

❖ Studying

- *"Study to shew thyself approved unto God, a workman that needeth not to be ashamed, rightly dividing the word of truth."* **2 Timothy 2:15**

    Studying can help you retain up to 50% of content. Studying is the effort that you need to make as the next level from reading in order to understand, retain and utilise the information you have received. To study means to dig deeper into the subject matter.

❖ Memorise

- *Thy Word have I hid in mine heart that I might not sin against thee."* **Psalm 119:11**

    To memorise means you have stored what you have learnt through hearing and reading on your mind for use at the time of need. What you have memorised lives in your subconscious mind which can be easily retrieved.

❖ Meditating

- *"This book of the law shall not depart out of thy mouth; but thou shalt meditate therein day and night, that thou mayest observe to do according to all that is written therein: for then thou shalt make thy way prosperous, and then thou shalt have good success."* **Joshua 1:8**

    Meditation means that at this stage, you move what you know from your head to your heart and let it become part of your lifestyle.

To meditate effectively, you need to find some quiet time to think about what you have learnt, know and in the process your focus should not be distracted. It is through mediation that you receive the secrets of breakthrough and success for your future.

Grounded Spirituality

My father was born a Muslim but converted to Christianity during his university days. He was one of the very few Christians in his family and he raised all his children to be Christians. He never discriminated against other people's beliefs and religions. Of course, he always preferred everyone to join the Christian faith and he tried at every attempt to convert as many people as possible to the faith.

CHAPTER 6. Focus for Spiritual Success

My dad managed to raise all his children in the faith of Christianity and even now after his parting from the world over 20 years ago, I am still living and practising Christianity to this date. What my father did is commendable because even when we, his children, now discuss his memory, we know that the spiritual training we got from him with the support of our mothers, has been extremely influential in the way we live our lives now.

How did he get us focused on our spiritual success?

Every morning at 5a.m. he would wake everyone up for early morning prayers before he headed to the office. This was a normal routine in our house without fail. This is the time that he used to teach us about the word and principles of God. Also, for two weeks in the month of August we used to attend Mount Taborah(A Church of The Lord (Aladura) annual worldwide retreat) for fasting and prayers. He used this period to train and discipline us in the way of the Lord. Though at the time I did not understand why he did what he did in the way that he did it, I am now truly grateful for all that he did.

Going by *1 Timothy 2:14* (the Bible passage above), which gives the instruction for you to lead by good example, my father lead his family by a good spiritual example because he was always at the morning prayers, and he fasted with us when he instructed us to fast. If my father hadn't lived by example, I don't think that I would still be standing in my faith now. It was his teaching and belief in God that has seen me through most of the challenges I have experienced in life.

Teach them when they are young

How many families make the time to pray together now? Do you have the time to read, study or even meditate on the word? Do you have the time to teach the next generation and guide them for spiritual success?

As Pastor Yemisi Ashmiolo would say "you've got to catch them when they are young." You need to start focusing the next generation for spiritual success when they are young, and the younger the better. The evolution presents us with challenges now that, if the next generation do not have a focus on their spiritual success, they may miss their entire destiny.

No matter who you are, you need a spiritual being that you can report to, commune with and fellowship with. Ask any successful person and you will know that they all have a spiritual authority or at least practice the principles that attract success.

What will help your next generation focus on their spiritual development is that they see you, their leaders, practicing what you teach. Your next generation need to have a deep understanding of what they are being taught and what the benefits of having a focus on spiritual success means for them. The root and the foundation of everything is what determines the fruits that it will germinate. If they are rooted well, then they will succeed in life.

Youths have to understand what benefits they have to gain in the spiritual contents. They need know why they believe in what they believe in in-order to be able to defend themselves anywhere confidently knowing the facts they are standing on. If they do not have the facts, then their spirituality may not be sound and can therefore easily be taken from them and ultimately be replaced with another belief. It is what they understand that they will follow.

It is very important that your next generation have a desire and aspiration to develop as they proceed in their spiritual journey. The next generation must be challenged with spiritual goals that they have identified by themselves. They should also be in the position to express their thought process and determine how they are going to achieve their spiritual goals.

How many of you are just going to your places of worship every week without having spiritual development goals and aspirations. And at the end of every year you find yourself in the same position as when you started at the beginning of that year. If you are finding yourself at the end of the year, in the same place as you were at the beginning of the year, then this means you have not experienced spiritual growth in that year.

In order to attain spiritual success, you will need to set yourself goals and work out the action steps that you need to take in order to achieve this goal. The TNCG coaching service can support you in identifying your spiritual development goals and actions you need to take in order to achieve them. www.TheNextChosenGeneration.com.

Chapter 7

Focus for Academic Success

CHAPTER 7
Focus for Academic Success

"Education is our passport to the future, for tomorrow belongs to the people who prepare for it today." **Malcolm X**

My daughter had just finished year 5 and it was during the summer holidays, when a friend asked me "Is your daughter taking the 11+ exams", I looked at her puzzled, not really knowing what she was asking me. I think that through the expression on my face, she might have guessed I didn't know what she was talking about. Actually, I had heard of the 11+, but I didn't fully understand it and the benefits it would have for my children. It was not until this conversation that I realised how beneficial it was.

My friend continued and said "If your daughter is going into year 6, then you should be preparing her for 11+. 11+ is the exam they need to take, so that they can get into a good grammar school." I gave no response, as I had obviously not done my research in this area.

When I got home from work that evening, I went on the internet to look into the 11+ exams and the grammar schools. The next day I begged my sister to work with my daughter for the exam, as I didn't know where I could get a teacher from. The exams where in November so we had just 4 months to prepare. Unfortunately, I didn't realise at the time that some parents had started preparing their children for this exam as early as when their children were in year 3 and 4 (2-3 years prior). When I saw the exam paper, I knew we had our work cut out for us that summer. As it goes, my daughter didn't pass the exam and she missed out on the opportunity to attend the best government funded education available.

My son was to take the same exam one year later. As we prepared him for this exam, I knew once again we had left things a little late

CHAPTER 7. Focus for Academic Success

and to be quite honest with you, I was in panic mode throughout the whole year. You'd actually think he was preparing to sit his PhD the way that I way I was carrying on.

Finally he sat the examination that we had prepared for. The night before the exam results came through; I was sat in front of my laptop till midnight waiting for the results and the verdict of whether he had gotten into grammar school of our choice. The results didn't come till the very early hours of the morning. He had made the cut of mark but not well enough to gain admission. Prior to the release of these results though, he had sat the common entrance for a private school. Thankfully, he had passed and gained admission to the private school which we had registered him for at the last minute. So all was not lost.

However, on the day we received he's 11+ exam results, I had never been so disappointed in myself before in my life. I was depressed, angered and frankly thought I must be a useless mum for not knowing the education system enough in order to get my children into the best education facility. I felt lost and cheated by the system. I remember the following morning as I was in the bathroom; I just sat at the corner of the bath and broke down in tears.

That same week I was to attend the 2011 Mother's Summit programme that was being held in North West London hosted by Pastor Funke Felix Adejumo. To be quite honest with you, I didn't want to go because as usual I blamed God for not raising my awareness in time for my children to pass the 11+. However, through the encouragement of my husband, I went to this event, though I was crying and wallowing in self-pity all the way.

When I arrived at the event, little did I know that God had lined up Mrs. Yemisi Akindele to be one of the speakers at this event. Mrs. Akindele is the internationally known CEO of High Achievers Academy. She had spoken for about 20mins about the educational system in the UK and the importance of good education for our children. I asked myself, did God bring her here just for me? After the event, I was amongst the crowd of women that surrounded her, with a billion and one questions to ask her and take her contact details. I knew my conversation with her, was not for that environment so I just took her number and decided to call her the following Monday.

For the rest of the weekend, I couldn't sleep. Something told me that she would have a solution for me. Monday morning finally came and I thought I would be the first person to call her. I was wrong because by the time I called her, her phone was busy and it turned out that I needed to call her about 8 times before I finally got to speak with her.

The first thing I said to her after the usual greeting was "My children failed the 11+ what do I do now?" I honestly thought, she was going to tell me that it was too late that there was nothing she could do for me, but she replied and said "Don't worry, there's always 13+". "What? 13+ What do you mean by 13+?" I replied. Mrs. Akindele went on to educate me about 13+ exams and other opportunities associated with this.

Following our conversation, without a doubt on my mind, both my daughter and my son enrolled on her summer programme. Through her knowledge, expertise, teaching and transformational teaching both my children ended up in boarding school where they were they have been given the opportunity to become high achievers.

From this time onwards, I knew that I couldn't afford this kind of mistake in the life of my children again if I wanted them to be successful. I therefore decided to make education, career and business opportunities for the next generation a focus for me and got to know the system in all these areas. When, I say I got to know the system, I mean I got to know the system. I figured out that if I wanted my children to be truly successful, then I would have to find out as much as possible in order for me to be able to guide and support them in making the right decisions for their future.

CHAPTER 7. Focus for Academic Success

What follows below is all that I know is available to the next generation of children, youths and young adults in the UK at present.

If you do not living in the UK, my advice to you is that you get to know the educational opportunity available in your country so that you can offer your child / children the best you can, according to your abilities and capabilities. This may mean that you have to step out of your comfort zone and make some sacrifices. I can assure you, it will all be worthwhile in the end.

The UK Educational System

The UK has a mix of private and public educational institutions offering academic learning facilities to children from the age of 4. From this age children under go different levels of assessments through the government set key stages. The four key stages are as follows:

Key Stage 1	Ages 5-7	Years 1 and 2
Key Stage 2	Ages 7-11	Years 3, 4, 5 and 6
Key Stage 3	Ages 11-14	Years 7, 8 and 9
Key Stage 4	Ages 14-16	Years 10 and 11

It is during key stage 2 (beginning of years 6) that children who intend to attend grammar schools will need to sit the 11+ exam as an entry exam for these schools.

The only time children can enter a grammar school is at 11+ and 16+. However if a space becomes available due to someone leaving the school and your child is on the school's waiting list, then your child may be invited or not taking up their offered place for a further assessment in-order to be given this space. So if your child has missed out on the opportunity to gain attendance into grammar school at the first attempt. It is worth you putting their name on the school's waiting list for any future opportunities that may arise.

Common entrance, will also be sat for entry into private schools at this stage. Most private schools offer scholarships and bursaries especially for children that are gifted and talented at the 11+ entry level and a few will give scholarships prior to this age.

11+ is not the only time that you can gain admission or scholarship to private schools in the UK. There is also an opportunity to enter at 13+ and 16+ but the competition becomes tougher at these stages age.

Previously in the UK, youths could legally leave the education system in the UK with or without good grades. However, recently this age has been increased to 18 with Maths and English being key for continuation.

If your child decides to proceed through the education system from 16+, then they do so by following the educational process below:

GCSE is the General Certificate of Secondary Education. A system of public exams taken in various subjects from the age of about 16. These subjects are normally chosen between the age of 13-14 allowing 2-3 years for the completion of the certification.

IGCSE is the International General Certificate of Secondary Education. It is academically challenging but internationally used in order to prepare students for the International Baccalaureate, A' Levels and BTEC Level 3.

A 'Level is the Advanced Level of subjects taken in school. A' Levels are normally taken following the achievement of GCSEs or IGCSE and is used as the qualification for entrance into university. It normally takes two years to complete this level of education.

International Baccalaureate (IB) is an alternative to A' Level for students aged 16-19. It is an internationally recognized academic qualification that can be completed by students all over the world. The IB leads to the a qualification known as the IB Diploma, which is recognized and respected by Universities. The IB is a useful qualification especially if you are planning for your child to study abroad.

The **Cambridge Pre-U** is a post-16 qualification that prepares students for degree courses at universities. This qualification is considered to be academically superior to A-level in terms of breadth of study, skill and the level of independence that a student requires in order to obtain the top marks in those qualifications.

It is only the top public schools (fee paying) and very few grammar schools in the UK that run the Cambridge Pre-U Qualification. *Cambridge International Examinations (Website), 2015*

Business and Technology Educational Council (BTEC) and General National Vocational Qualification (GNVQ) are also alternative qualification to A' Levels. They are vocational qualifications. The BTEC and GNVQ are extended diploma that offers a secondary school leaving qualification and vocational qualification. The BTEC is available in England, Wales and Northern Ireland. These qualifications can be taken at any age from 16 as an entry qualification into some Universities.

Diploma of Higher Education (DipHE) is a higher education qualification in the United Kingdom. It is awarded after two years of full-time study at a university or other higher education institution.

First Degree can be in the form of Bachelor of Arts (BA) or Bachelor of Science (BSc). This is normally obtained from registered and recognized University institutes all over the world. Entry age is normally around 18/19 and course duration is normally between 3-4 years and can be longer depending on the type of degree the student is taking.

It is worth taking the time to look into the Russell Group (24 Leading Universities in the UK) and Red Brick (British Universities founded in the late 19th and early 20th centuries in major cities)

Universities. You can find out more about the Russell Group Universities by visiting www.russellgroup.ac.uk.

Masters is the next level of academic attainment following the completion of the First degree. This can be completed as Masters of Arts (MA), Masters of Science (MSc) and Masters of Business Administration (MBA). A student that is willing to commit to this level of education is looking at a minimum of 1 additional year at University following the completion of the first degree. I say a minimum of 1 year because it can be extended if the student requires additional time to complete their thesis.

PHD / DBA / Doctorate can be completed following the attainment of a Master's degree (There may be exemption opportunities). This level of academic excellence demonstrates the talent of the student and their desire to gain knowledge. This level of education opens doors in the academic industry and can provide an individual with a competitive edge in the employment sector, especially for research related jobs. There are some jobs out there that have this level of education as their minimum requirement.

As youths progress through the educational process, they are likely to find each stage challenging and most definitely more challenging than the previous level they have just completed. If they are finding their current stage of studies challenging, they don't need to give up, instead they can seek for extra tuition from organisations such as the High Achievers. They can also be coached in-order to ensure they remain goal focused to achieve success. Some schools, Colleges and Universities also sometimes put on extra support classes for selected subjects which are worth considering.

It is important to note that planning ahead as much as possible is important as the subjects and the grades attainted from GCSE and A' Level can have an effect on the University you get into. For example, if you are aiming for your child to attain a place in one of the Russell group Universities, you need to consider the fact that a minimum of two out of the below subjects are required for consideration/admission:

- Maths
- Physics
- Chemistry
- English Literature or English Language
- History
- Latin
- French
- German
- Economics

Excel in Key Subjects, August 2015.

Education is a very important factor in the development of your children and they should be encouraged to achieve their best and for them to obtain the highest level possible in order for them to gain a competitive edge whatever they do. Education will also more likely present them with more opportunities in the future, especially as the race for success becomes more challenging.

Going through the academic root for success may not be as challenging as it was before. The courses on offer at different universities all over the world presents some great opportunities for youths who do not desire to study traditional courses. Whatever it is your next generation desires to study, it is recommended that you do some research before you conclude that it doesn't exist or it's not worthwhile. You'll be surprised at what is currently available at Universities.

If you are challenged with the opportunities of course options and you need support in making the right university choices contact www.TheNextChosenGeneration.com for the coaching experience that will focus you on the right choice.

Chapter 8

Focus for Employment Success

CHAPTER 8
Focus for Employment Success

I never thought I'd see the day. The last exam for my Bachelor's degree was over. My dissertation was submitted. The labour and hard work over the last four years was going to finally yield the good fruit of a graduate management job. Well, so I thought until the job hunting started.

As I reviewed every suitable opportunity, I was shocked at potential employer's requirements which mostly said, "Must be a degree holder with at least 2 years relevant experience gained in the industry being applied for." I thought to myself, "Hey, hang on, how could I have experience in the industry when I've just finished my degree? I'm a degree holder applying for my first job in the corporate world. Surely the employers must understand that." It soon became obvious that they didn't, so I started to apply for non-management jobs and I was getting turned down for being over-qualified. "Hello!!! Can somebody help me here?"

When I started my degree four years earlier, I was made aware that employers were employing graduates just for being a graduate. By the time I graduated, the situation had changed because there were now more graduates on the job market. A simple case of supply and demand that didn't help many graduates in my position back then. "God help me," I often prayed "what do I do now?"

I remembered when I was 16, my dad had suggested that I attend a secretarial vocational course in order to gain typing skills. I turned his offer down because I thought he wanted me to become his secretary, as he had done to my elder sisters. I remember telling him that I won't need the skills because when I grow up, I'm going to be as rich as him and hire someone to do that for me. He grinned and let me be.

As a fresh graduate and in the absence of no corporate opportunities that gave me my own personal secretary and no funds to start a business that would pay me a good wage, let alone a personal secretary, I enrolled on a four-week Microsoft Office course to learn how to use all the MS Office tools and how to speed type. If only I had listened to my dad all those years ago. At least, I would be able to speed type now. The course was done all in the name of obtaining a job as a Project Administrator as this became the only avenue for me to get into the job market.

It was about two years after working as a Project Administrator, when I started applying for managerial roles that I discovered that there was so much more that I could have done as an undergraduate that would have given me a better chance in the employment world following graduation. I discovered that I could have done the Duke of Edinburgh awards, which is highly valued by employers. The Duke of Edinburgh Awards are still available today. There is also now the National Community Service (NCS) training that employers welcome on the CV of young recruits.

One of the coaching programs that I deliver to youths is the MAGIC program. MAGIC provides young people the opportunity to develop a wide range of crucial life skills that can be used immediately after completing the program. MAGIC stands for:

- Motivation
- Assertiveness
- Goal Achievement
- Initiative
- Confident Communication

This program is designed to complement both formal and informal education and provides a way for young people to explore and enhance their own development. The program is approved and accredited by the Open College Network.

According to The Coaching Academy, Employers have also began to show a preference in hiring young people with this coaching experience.

Below are a few suggestions of what youths can do whilst studying in-order to have an advantage in the employment world before or after graduation from their first degree.

Internship

Internships provide direct work experience in a specific role/s to students who are currently studying for their first degrees. The program normally offers summer work placements or 1 year work placements to students prior to the completion of their first degree. The duration of the internship is dependent on the industry sector and the employer.

This is a good option for youths that know what they want to do and which industry they desire to work in. It is also a good way for the undergraduate to gain valuable work experience whilst getting to know the company.

Employers normally use internships to assess the capabilities of a student. There have been cases in the past where employers have offered their interns full-time employment following the completion of their degree.

Apprentice

A financial impact in the education system over recent years is the introduction of university fees in the UK. This has led to a shift in the thinking and decision-making of many students leaving school from the age of 16 or 18.

There is now an increase in school leavers that are opting the proposition of apprentice instead of paying somewhere in the region of £9,000 per academic year in tuition fees alone and, in some cases, additional expenses for accommodation etc... will also need to be factored in.

An apprenticeship is a system of training a new generation of the employment workforce via job-based training. This is normally accompanied by some classroom / reading and private studying. The employer is normally responsible for covering the cost of off-the-job training and the time that is required for training.

Apprentices are normally paid a lot less than graduates and their program of service normally lasts for 3-6 years depending on the employer.

Work Placement.

There are some organizations that are working with schools in order to offer work placements to students. For someone that is entering employment for the first time, this is not a bad place to start. Work placements are available to students from the age of 16 and can last for anything between 2weeksto a couple of months, depending on the employer.

Graduate Employment Scheme

There are a lot of companies now that recruit fresh or recent graduates for a program of work. This normally operates in a similar way to an internship and can last from between 12 – 24months depending on the employer. The roles that are presented to the people on the scheme are entry employment roles that need to be occupied by a graduate.

It's the time frame attached to this scheme that differentiates it from normal employment.

Graduate Jobs

Graduate jobs work in the same way as full-time employment, except there might be a working period attached to the contract. Following the completion of this period, the contract is reviewed and the graduate employee has the prerogative to continue employment with that organization or not. However, the rules are quite different depending on individual companies.

Full Time Employment

Full-time employment means that you are a regular employee with no additional or restrictive conditions attached to your contract of employment.

Voluntary Employment

Consideration could be given to voluntary employment, especially in the absence of none. It is better to be in one employment or the other, than to not have work at all. Voluntary employment can be done full- or part-time. The word "voluntary" usually means you will not be rewarded with payment but some organizations will offer you paid expenses.

For career and transition coaching visit,
www.TheNextChosenGeneration.com.

Chapter 9

Focus for Business Success

CHAPTER 9
Focus for Business Success

The cost of tuition, coaching and possibly school/university fees can seem to be quite high and financially draining. In order to meet these financial obligations in trying to achieve the best for your child and in order to present youths with the opportunity to make some income without putting their studies at risk. I have listed 20 business opportunities below for you to consider for generating your main income or earning as extra income that you may need to support the financing of the development of your child.

Raising children in the current economic climax can be challenging, especially with access to little funds. The lack of, or not enough money may limit the opportunities that youths can have. The current economic status of the world and the evolution of technology presents you with opportunities to diversify to different areas of making money. Often the youths I work with ask me about how they can get jobs, so I spent my time coaching some of them to write or polish up their CVs and prepare them for interviews. However, over the recent years I have come to the realization that starting a business in what they are gifted in, may be an even better idea than getting a job. There are business opportunities out there now available to parents and youths that may generate funds and sometimes more that you would get from your usual employment

The use of the PCs, iPads, laptops and smart phones has opened opportunities to do business on the go or in the comfort of our own home. This can be done through the internet. If you are new to the world of internet business, I would encourage you to attend one of the courses offered by the Internet Business School (IBS) in the UK. IBS can also deliver via online learning platforms for those who are not in the position to attend their live training events. They have a variety of courses that are suitable for the people who:

CHAPTER 9. Focus for Business Success

- Want to learn more about how to make money online
- Are an existing business owners wanting to learn how to create online presence and increase your profits
- Are start-up entrepreneurs
- Are experts wishing to increase their income.

If at least one of the above applies to you, then I highly recommend that you contact the Internet business school at www.focusedinternetmarketing.com.

The idea of starting a business may sound daunting because of the business plan you need to prepare, the funds you need to raise, the time and effort you need to put into it and much more. However, if you start by taking small steps to achieve your business goal, you will realise that it is all worthwhile, especially if you have taken the time to do things properly. If you are doing the right business for you, with determination, skill, support and focus you will be successful.

Below are a few opportunity options that you can consider engaging with in order to generate additional income or develop into your main source of income.

1. Acting or Extra on TV set: If you like watching soaps or movies, why not become a part of it instead of just watching it all the time. You can get involved by becoming an actor or if your acting is not that great you can become an extra on the set. I hear you can make up to £150 / day. Whether you aspire to be an actor or an extra on a TV set, you will need be registered with an agency.

2. Affiliate marketing: Some companies know this as a way to do their marketing. This means that you get a commission for every customer you introduce to the company. There are now a lot of companies that offer affiliate marketing through the internet and it is therefore advisable for you to know the product and company that you wish to promote.

3. Auction Websites: These are a good place to auction products that you may want to buy or sell using an auction method.

4. Translation Services: If you are fortunate enough to know more than one language including English, then I would recommend that you offer your services to organizations who are calling out for this type of service. You can also advertise on sites such as Odesk.

5. Party and Events Management: This has become one of the fastest growing industries as people love to celebrate a lot. Parties can range from children's parties to adult milestone parties. Events are big business. You will need excellent organizational, communication and interpersonal skills in order to be really successful as this role can be challenging and demanding.

I used to run an events company part-time but I found it was too demanding for someone like me that holds a full-time job and had three children to raise alongside church and other voluntary activities. However, for the short period that I got involved in this, I enjoyed myself and the challenges that some customers brought to me. It could have become very big but I did it more as a hobby than real business, which I guess that was the down-fall of the business. If you are doing business, you've got to be in it to make profit.

6. Internet Selling on Amazon and eBay: You no longer need a shop to sell your products. You can now purchase your products and sell them via Amazon and eBay. By doing this you are exposing yourself to an international market as opposed to a local or national audience.

7. Childcare Services: This is one business that is not going to go bust any time soon. As more people are having children and more parents are going to work, the demand for childcare is on the increase. Childcare services can include but are not limited to breakfast and afterschool clubs, baby-sitting and child-minding.

CHAPTER 9. Focus for Business Success

8. Rent a space in your home: I heard recently on the news that people are now renting out their parking space especially in the London area where there is conjunction charges. Other space that you can rent out is a room and your garage as storage.

9. Rent your Home for movies: Film-makers are sometimes on the lookout for homes to rent for their movies. You can offer your home for this service. By doing this, you can charge £500 upwards per day depending on the type of house and location.

10. DJ at parties: Every party needs music otherwise it won't be a party. This is a nice earning if you have the flare for this.

11. Musician: If you are talented in music or play an instrument very well, you can offer your services to bands, churches or other religious communities. You may also want to consider playing live at parties and other social events.

12. Rate music: I recently found out that you can listen to music, rate it and get paid for doing so. If music is your thing, this is a nice little earner.

13. Makeup and beauty services: Makeup artists are definitely making the money now. Every special event will be looking for someone to provide this service. Events could be proms, milestone birthdays, weddings and general public appearances.

14. Website Designer: The new way of doing business for any company that wants internet presence, they are going to need a webpage, which needs to be done by people that know what they are doing. If you are good in this field, why not offer your services to people you know or advertise yourself on the internet.

15. Mystery shopper / Traveller: There are companies that now hire people to be mystery shoppers or travellers. This means that they pay you to use their services in order to rate the quality of what their staff are delivering. The companies then use your collected data to improve their services. I believe that Airline,

Restaurants, Shops and even online sites, such as Amazon, are into this now.

16. Selling used items: Why not have a look around your home and see if there is anything that you no longer have use of. Put them together and sell them through car sales, garage sales or directly to organizations that are ready to pay good money for them. Items could include, but are not limited to, books, clothes and other products.

17. Coaching / Teaching: Coaching and teaching services can be offered in any area of expertise. If you have attained a certain level of education, then you can teach in that particular subject at levels lower than what you have achieved. For coaching, you can develop your coaching skills in sports, health & fitness, business, personal and career. There are more areas that you can consider coaching, but these you will have to explore based on your personal interest.

18. Network Marketing: you can register with companies like Avon, Forever Living and other health, beauty and makeup products, especially as these have been designed via a catalogue order through a representative like yourself.

19. Book writing: If you have a particular interest, talent or experience in a particular subject, then you may consider writing a book. This is a good way to share your knowledge with members of the public that may not be easily accessible to you or the information available to you.

I am writing this book now and to be quite honest with you, I didn't think that I could write a book neither did I want to write a book until last year when I went to a business conference and whilst one of the speakers was on stage he said "You have a message inside you, go and write a book." I thought he was talking to me, but of course he was talking to the whole room. However, I saw it as a challenge and here I am writing this book.

20. Public Speaking: If you have a gift that allows you to talk in front of small, medium or large groups, then you should consider public speaking. If you like to talk, want to present or sell to a group of people, then public speaking is a good way to make money whilst on stage.

My first experience as a public speaker took place when I was about 9 years old. It was the annual spring school play. My class had the challenge of performing the story about the hare and the tortoise. Once the script was written out, the drama gave out all the parts of the play and for one moment I thought "fluke, I don't have a part." All of a sudden, she called me, "Juliet, you will be LADY JULIET". Where did she get that from? There was no Lady Juliet in the story." I thought to myself as the whole class looked around in confusion. "It seems the drama teacher is starting to get creative", I said.

My role in the school play as LADY JULIET meant that I would have to act and speak like Margret Thatcher on stage and present the winning award to the tortoise. Wow how exciting.

On the night of the play, I got up on stage all poshly dressed wearing a skirt suit that my mum bought for me, looking like Margret Thatcher. I said my lines without any hiccups. As I completed my scene, the audience which was mixed with parents and teachers, and the headmaster stood up and applauded. I was thrilled. When I got off stage, the first thing the drama teacher said to me was, "you're a natural. Well done."

This is where public speaking started for me, though at the time I didn't realize that public speaking was going to become a lifetime career.

If you have the talent to speak confidently to a group of people or you want to have the talent, then I would encourage you to pick on this growing career market as a public speaker. There are now training institutions that offer great training in this field.

Recognizing my talent and my desire to help people achieve their goals and objectives, I now offer services as a public speaker. To find out more about my speaking services, please visit www.YetundeAdeshile.com.

Other Business Ventures

There are many more business ventures out there and you will have to explore them as much as possible in order for you to identify what's best for you and your family. There are rules and regulations governing running your own business and you will need to explore these in order to make sure that you are making the right decision. You will more than likely need a business plan and some capital. There are a few organizations that can provide business start-up grants and support for the people who have the right initiatives.

If you would like a longer list of business opportunities, please email your request to enquiries@TheNextChosenGeneration.com

Chapter 10

**Success –
No Matter What!**

CHAPTER 10
Success – No Matter What!

August 20th, 1992.

It is the early hours of the morning, the house phone rings. I pick up the phone. "Hello, hello. Oh good morning mummy".

"Yetunde, good morning. Can I speak to Titi?" mum replies is a disturbing tone.

"No, she went to Wales for the weekend," I replied.

"Ah. Ok. Is Bose there?" Mum asked.

"Yes ma, Auntie Bose is here". I replied.

At this point, I start to get worried. Mum hasn't said more than hello good morning, and we had not even had a short conversation before she's asking me to pass the phone to others. Obediently, I passed the phone to Auntie Bose (who is actually my cousin).

"Hello, good morning Ma," Auntie Bose said as she put the phone to her ears.

The next thing I heard was my mum breaking down in tears at the other end of the phone saying *"Baba tiku"* (Meaning Father is dead).

Auntie Bose shouted *"Baba tiku, baba wo?"* (*Baba wo*, meaning which father). Before Auntie Bose could ask another question, I grabbed the phone off her.

"Mum, what's the matter? What are you saying? I asked.

With tears and pain in her voice she replied" I'm sorry but your father passed away earlier on this morning".

The phone dropped from my hand. I froze for a while. No thoughts, no movement. I just froze. I didn't know what to say or do.

Auntie Titi (my elder sister) came back from Wales the following evening. I wasn't allowed to tell her anything until she got back from her weekend break. For days I didn't cry and I didn't have anything to say. I watched and listened as everyone arranged their travel to Nigeria for the funeral. I think it must have been on the third day, I was in the bath and I could hear my cousin and my sister talking about me. I starred in the air as memories of my father came gushing through my mind. For the first time since the news about his passing, I think reality hit me. I was never going to see my dad again. I felt pain, heart and disappointment. Why now? Why my dad? The realization that he wasn't going to be there for my graduation, wedding and to see my grandchildren was unimaginable. I broke down in tears. It took quite some time after that for the tears to stop.

It was almost the end of August and school was starting in September. Two weeks before daddy passed away, I had just managed to persuade him to allow me to go to the US for the furtherance of my education. What was going to happen to my plans? I hadn't made any plans to study anywhere else in the UK? Who is going to pay the school fees? What school would accept me at this last hour? I couldn't attend his funeral in Nigeria because I had to stay behind to sort out my education. After searching around going from one college to the other, I finally took the last space on offer at the local college down the road. Previously known as the North London College. It was walking distance from my sister's flat, so very convenient to get to.

I had chosen to fight for my future because I knew that even though my father was no longer with me physically, he would always remain in my heart. Secondly, I knew that my dad would have preferred me to focus on my education because that's the way he had brought me up. My life was already planned out long before I was old enough to make my own decisions, so even though he was no longer with me, I knew exactly what he would expect me to achieve.

Though there was joy in my heart that I had secured a college space, something told me that money wasn't going to be coming in a hurry for my fees. I had to get a job. One month ago, I had my whole life planned out. The following month it was all in shatters and I had to start all over again, in a completely different world. A world that I'm not used to or prepared for.

When I started the course, the classroom felt a bit weird and I knew it was going to take a while to make some new friends. This was made apparent as my dress sense and English accent were quite different. I not only struggled initially to make friends, but I couldn't even tell my current friends from boarding school where I was studying. On top of that, I had to find a job that would cover all expenses. It was a different way of learning and definitely a different environment.

As the course progressed, studying became a challenge and I began to lose focus. This affected my performance and emotionally I was falling apart. Fortunately, my head tutor noticed that my performance wasn't as productive as he had expected (I think he was judging my performance based on the school I went to). He called me into his office for a discussion.

"Juliet, is everything alright?" Mr. Smith asked.

"Alright, what do you mean by alright?" I asked.

"Well, your grades, character and performance are very different from what I expected from the girl I interviewed about seven months ago," said Mr. Smith.

"In what way sir?" I asked.

"Well, for a girl with your educational standard, I would have hoped that you would be one of our best students." Mr. Smith said.

I just stared at him with my mouth opened, then it all just came out. I think I said something like "I need help sir."

"In what way?" he asked.

I told him the areas that I was struggling with the culture change of the educational institution. He in response told me about a mentoring programme that the college was involved with in partnership with some local organisations. He asked me to join the programme as he felt it may help me cope better. I jumped at this opportunity because I knew I needed some support to get me through the course. Thankfully, I was allocated a mentor that had a positive impact on my studying and supported me for the remainder of my studies.

Earlier in chapter 1, I made mention to a study that stated that young people shut down quickly especially when they feel they cannot achieve their goals. After my dad passed away, for the first few days, that's what I did. However, I knew I had to bounce back quickly because my whole life was ahead of me. At the time, no education meant no future. I had no choice but to keep going until I achieved my goal. My father's death meant all my plans had to change, but I found a way out and every step of the way God was always there for me. Today, I'm a graduate with a post graduate master's degree and running my own businesses. The journey has been challenging, but being focused on the end result gave me the results that I desired.

Success comes with pain and sacrifices, but everything you give it, makes it worthwhile once you achieve it. Focus on your success, no matter what. Do whatever it takes (within reason) to achieve your success. Don't stop trying until you achieve your goal. Don't shut down or give up. It is always important that you know what you are doing and when, so that when life throws you what you don't plan for or expect, you can bounce back to reality and get back on track.

I am challenging you to do things for yourself. Work smart and hard, look for the right opportunities, talk to the right people. Ask and make sure that you get the right support in order to achieve your goals.

In order to be an achiever in life, you must believe in yourself because it's your beliefs that determine your end result. Someone once taught me that "believe" stands for the following:

Build
Empower
Limit
Inspire
Evidence
False
Self-Talk

Whatever you believe yourself to be is what shapes all of the above which can in turn give you a positive or a negative outcome in life. Coaching can support the elimination of limiting beliefs.

Perhaps you are thinking that success is not for you. I want to assure you that success is for everyone. You have a gift, you have a purpose and a goal that only you can achieve. I want you to take some time (as long as you like) to meditate on the following carefully. Once you understand this, you will realise that you have your own purpose and calling which you must achieve in order to be considered successful.

> *"God has put a dream inside you. It's yours and no one else's. It declares your uniqueness. It holds your potential. Only you can live it. Not to discover it, take responsibility for it and act upon it is to negatively affect yourself as well as all those who would benefit from your dream."* **John Maxwell, 2015.**

A couple of years ago, I had the opportunity to mentor a couple of secondary school girls. When I first met these girls, they both came across as intelligent and reasonably well-behaved. The challenge they were both facing was they were not achieving the grades that they could potentially achieve in school. They had both just started their year ten (In the UK, this is the academic year prior to their GCSE's). Through the mentoring sessions, I had to switch to coaching halfway as I felt I didn't have the same life

CHAPTER 10. Success - No Matter What!

experience that they did, neither were they aspiring to do what I did. Therefore mentoring might not have been the right approach for them.

At the time I started the mentoring programme, Sharon and Olivia were both achieving grades in the region of D/Es. During one of our sessions we had looked at the opportunities that they had ahead of them following the completion of their GCSEs. Using coaching type questions, both Sharon and Olivia were challenged to review their present self and imagine where they wanted to be following the completion of their GCSEs. By doing this, they realised that their current performance wasn't good enough for them to achieve their goal of progressing to college in order to progress in their chosen career. During the sessions, they were able to identify their goals and what they needed to do in order to achieve them. The best thing was that they both came to the conclusion that in order to achieve their goals, they couldn't continue to perform the same way that they had been performing. Following all these realisations, they came up with their own actions which they wanted to take in order to help them achieve their goals. Surprisingly, their proposed actions included setting two hours for homework every weekday evening, switching off all gadgets (including mobile phone) during homework time and spending less time socializing.

They both stuck to their action plan and within 3 months their grades changed drastically. I remember Sharon bringing her exam paper to one of the sessions to prove to me what grade she had achieved in math which she didn't particularly like. To be quite honest with you, I don't think she thought she could achieve an A in math. She even shocked her teacher.

About 3 years ago, John was in his 2nd year of University barely making the grades to graduate with good results that would get him the employment that he wanted at the completion of his course. John had the desire to become an engineer. During his coaching sessions, it had come to light that John lacked self-confidence, so I used the subsequent coaching sessions to focus on supporting him in breaking his thought patterns and become more positive. The other sessions were used to clearly define his goals and produce actions plans that would enable him to achieve these goals. John is now a graduate that achieved a 1st class (Hons) degree and he is working in a prestigious job that is considered to be quite good for a fresh graduate.

Mentoring and coaching that incorporates the best support techniques have helped me to achieve what I needed to achieve so far in life. This is one of the reasons why I love supporting the next generation through pastoring, mentoring and coaching.

In life, you've got to know what you want and how to get it. You need to focus on the end goal and use every opportunity available to you wisely. You can sometimes be faced with challenges, but you can overcome these with the right person supporting you. It is important to find a neutral person that won't judge or put unnecessary pressure you, but they will work with you in line with what you want to achieve and positively support you all the way. It's your life and therefore it's your call what you make of it.

As one of my coaches says "You can overcome every obstacle, no matter what". What areas of life are you finding challenging? Coaching is available to you in order to support your development and help you overcome your challenges.

Chapter 11

The Evolution Is In Your Hand

CHAPTER 11

The Evolution Is In Your Hand

Focus on the Youths.

I was just getting up from my knees following the completion of my morning devotion when I heard a voice saying "Focus on your children!" I looked around my room and thought to myself "what?" The voice came again, "Focus on your children."

Days and weeks passed and I kept on thinking, "Focus on your children", what could this mean? As far as I was concerned, my children were doing fine. Well, so it seemed. No meaning came to me, so I decided that maybe a family retreat would help. Fortunately, my husband agreed for us to head to Longleat for a long weekend.

It was during this weekend that I discovered that "focus on your children" meant spending more quality time with your children. The time we had spent together at Longleat helped us as a family to build better relationships with each other. I developed my listening skills which led to me understanding my children more. As a result of this outcome, I am now more involved in my children's lives which gives me the privilege to guide them appropriately with their decisions. I also have a better understanding of their interests.

The results that my children gained from this experience, is that they are better at what they do and they are improving every day. There was a gap in my parenting relationship with my children before, but now things are a lot better than they were. I still maintain a good knowledge of what they are up to and into. It has improved so much that at the last parent meeting that I attended with my daughter, Rachael, we stood outside one of the classrooms chatting and she said to me "Mum, I'm glad you went on this spiritual journey."

Naturally I looked at her in astonishment and replied "What do you mean by that?" "You are a better mum now than you were before," she replied. Our conversation went on and it came to light that it was when I took on the role of youth pastor in church that I began to change as a mum. God had somehow used this role to help me become a better mum to my children and to rediscover my purpose and passion. God had also used the ministry to change me to become a better listener and teacher.

To focus on the next generation means that in your different areas of leadership or responsibility, especially as a parent, you need to take the necessary time out to understand the youth you are responsible for. As one of Stephen R Covey's 7 habits from his book, *The 7 Habits of Highly Effective People* says "Seek first to understand and then to be understood." Take the time and have the courage to understand them first, so that your relationship can be better developed.

Focusing on the next generation means to understand their world, the challenges that youths are presented with and knowing the best way to help them to overcome these challenges. For example, their exposure to technology. You as a parent or youth leader, should not shy away from technology developments, but instead embrace it with open arms, get involved with it. Know it well enough to guide them through the risks and opportunities that it brings. Understand them in totality and embrace the new developing culture and change they will be brought up to adapt to.

I challenge you to do whatever it takes to focus on the next generation the way you know best. I challenge you to take the first step in the process by changing yourself in order to improve the future of the next generation.

Take a new approach to raising the next generation.

"The significant problems we face cannot be solved at the same level of thinking we were at when we created them." Einstein.

I want you to go back and read the quote above from Einstein's observation. Now pause for a moment. Look around and within you. Answer the following questions:

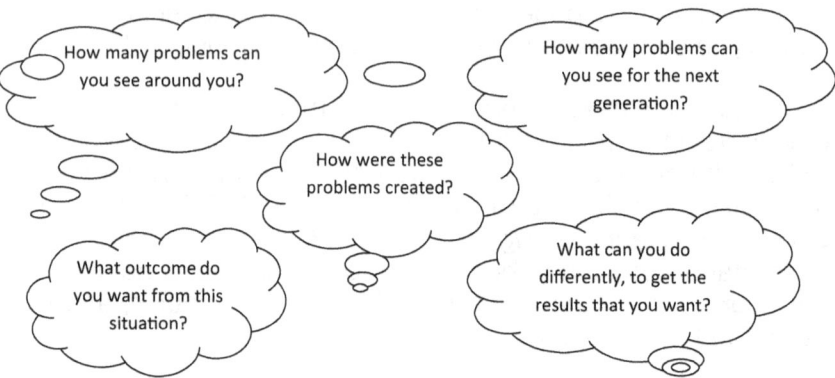

It was question time during the 2012 RCCG Good Women's Fellowship Annual Conference in the UK, hosted by Pastor Folu Adeboye. I can't clearly remember the question that was asked, but I can remember the answer that Pastor Folu Adeboye gave. She said "Take a new approach." This answer has stuck on my mind since I heard her say that. It's what I do whenever I come across situations that seem to be one of those that can move you forward or backwards. As TD Jakes would say, "Your grinding phase." I ask myself the above questions and look at the new approach that I can take in order to achieve my end goal. This is not just for personal development, but used in my career and businesses as well. The problems that we have created by doing what we do best can only be resolved with a new way of thinking and behaving so that we can achieve the best results.

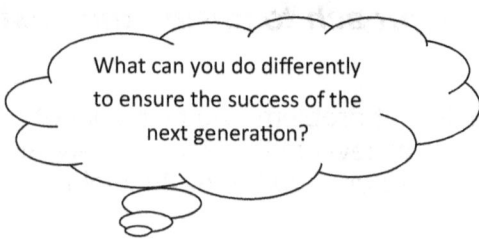

CHAPTER 11. The Evolution Is In Your Hands

Raising the next generation requires a different skill set that you may not have. Do whatever it takes, no matter what, in order to secure their success. A new approach that can be applied is parent coaching and youth coaching as a support system to be focused for success. For more information, visit: www.TheNextChosenGeneration.com.

Flow with the change

Would you agree with me that you cannot continue to do things the same way you have always done it and expect a different result. What I mean is that you will need to change in order to get a different result from what you are achieving now, if your results are not moving you in the right direction.

You as leaders in the capacity as parents, teachers, head teachers, community leaders, government leaders and any other leadership positions that are responsible for developing the next generation, you will need to start developing a different mind-set if you haven't already done so. Your mind-set will need to change in line with the matters that the youth evolution presents society with today because it is when you do this that you will be in the position to provide your next generation with the help and support that they need in order to achieve success.

Note that those who flow with change rather than resist it are less stressed, healthier and happier.

You are a leader for the next generation, especially if you fall into the categories of parents, teachers, employers, mentors or coaches. Therefore, you all have a role to play in developing the next generation's progress and securing their future success.

Whether you are a leader at home, school, church, community or in a group, you must keep learning and developing yourself in line with the evolution because this will lead to your growth and empower you to make a more effective impact on the next generation.

The ability to lead is a skill that comes naturally to some but not to all, but one which can be learned and improved. The challenges presented to us for leading the next generation means that you're learning process is ongoing in order to keep up with the times. It's not just to keep up, but to be ahead, otherwise you run the risk of losing the next generation to the evolution, or potentially, they might lose you.

I came across the following reading in a daily devotional by United Christian Broadcasters (UCB) and felt it may be worthwhile sharing it with you:

> *"Think how foolish it is to pray for success, and resist the changes needed to bring it about. However, we do that, don't we? Let's face it; it's easier to settle for the status quo than to face the "what ifs" that accompany progress. Some of us even think it's selfish and unspiritual to pray for success."* **(Word for Today, 2015).**

Everybody that I know and probably, some people that I do not know, want to and do pray for success. You know you want success, you know you want success for your next generation and the generation after that. However, you do not want to make the required changes in your life that will bring forth your success. Did you know that if you are not getting the results you want in your life doing what you are doing now, then you will need to do something different? It may be a very simple thing that you need to do differently or a big thing that you need to change. Whatever the case may be, there is something you will need to do in order to get the results that you desire.

CHAPTER 11. The Evolution Is In Your Hands

> *"Consider this list of "changes" you may be resisting: leaving an unfulfilling job, starting a business, or letting go of an unprofitable one, learning to use a computer, abandoning a toxic relationship, letting go of an unaffordable home, car, or lifestyle, establishing a responsible spending plan. All these changes are normal; they're not part of daily life. However, panic sets in when the change is unexpected."* **Word for Today, 2015.**

In order to achieve success, here are some steps you will need to take.

- Write down what success means to you.
- Then write down what this success means to you and your family, business or organisation.
- Make a list of what you think you will need to do differently in order to achieve your success.
- List any obstacles that you think may stop you from achieving this goal.

Once you have clearly done this exercise, now ask yourself, "Is this realistic and can I really do this no matter what?" If your answer is yes to both questions, then you have to or can go for your dream both for yourself and your next generation. You need to change everything necessary in order to make things happen the way you want them to.

One Voice

The Confederation of British Industry, in their 2012 report titled "A New Approach for Our Schools" states the following;

> *"It must be a priority for all of us - businesses as well as government and schools themselves to deliver the step change which will ensure that young people are*

> *fully equipped with the knowledge, skills, attitudes and attributes they need to succeed in work and life balance."*

The above quote is a reach out for help on behalf of the next generation to different leaders within their environment. Too much and often, they have been left to their own devices. Reports on the trend and crisis that youths are getting involved with, demonstrates that youths need support from people who are on their side, who will listen to their cry and work with them to make the best of the life that they have got.

The Conference of British Industry's report is calling out to you to join the force of making the change that is required to ensure the success of the next generation. This is not only applicable to just your personal next generation, but all the next generation that you have the opportunity to make a positive impact in their lives.

Yuma's their leader in any category as previously stated above, will need to prove and demonstrate that you believe in them and that you know that they are capable of achieving their dreams in order for them to gain a better chance of survival on the ladder of Success.

Schools need disciplined and focused children in school in order to ensure maximum impact. Parents need focused and disciplined children in order to live a peaceful and fulfilling life. The government is looking for the next generation that will present them with less challenges in the future. Employers are looking to employ a generation that are focused, who have acquired the right skills sets for the employment world.

Parents, teachers and communities, think for one moment what you could achieve with one voice for raising the next generation. With one voice and one purpose you form a powerful collective body of the greatest influencers that is responsible for raising the next generation. This means that you will be able to raise youths that are focused for success and therefore attain the goal of having disciplined and focused children in the community,

With one voice and the applied profession framework presented by coaching, you can expect to achieve the results that are now in great demand from the community, nation and the world.

Change is hard and challenging but you need to start somewhere to make it in order to achieve the results that you need and require. Expert coaching can support the change process that you are considering. Contact me for the coaching experience that will transform the way you do things in order to achieve the success that you want and desire for you and your next generation at: www.ThNextChosenGeneration.com.

The youth evolution is in your hands. What will you do with it?

THE NEXT CHOSEN GENERATION (TNCG)

TNCG is an organization that delivers mentoring and coaching for youths in order to support them in realizing their full potential and focus on success. TNCG also delivers parent coaching that supports the role of parenting in this modern day world.

Privately booked workshops and seminars can be delivered in schools, universities, corporate organization, charity organizations, religious groups, community organizations and private groups. www.TheNextChosenGeneration.com

The Next Chosen Generation (TNCG) Live Events
STEP UP™

This program will use mentoring and coaching skills over a course of seven sessions over a 3-day program, to empower youths to step up and rise to their full potential in order to achieve success. The Step Up™ program is designed to support youths in addressing the key influencing factors for securing the successful future they deserve. These factors are:

- Beliefs
- Discipline
- Opportunity
- Environment
- Choice
- Goals
- Focus

Focus to Achieve™

This is a 3-day boot camp that will present youth with possible options for their future. During these three days, youths will discover who they are and how they can improve themselves in order to keep ahead of the game. This program will be scheduled to run once during the school holidays.

This program is set to challenge and empower every youth that attends. There will be a positive change in the lives of every youth. The program will cover the following:

- Self-Awareness
- Setting Goals and Creating an Action Plan
- Decision Making and Choice
- School Options – GCSEs, A-Levels, Universities
- Career Options – Apprentice, Employment & Qualifications, Business Start-up
- Finance & Money Management
- Investment Options
- Relationship Matters
- Choice and Commitment

Parents Get Coached™

TNCG's Parent Coaching program is aimed at parents who are currently responsible for raising youths and want the best possible outcome for them and their children. Parents and Caretakers that complete the TNCG's parent coaching program increase the chances for their children's success, because the program will change the way they think and behave. The program aims to help parents support their youths during their transitional development phases.

The TNCG parent coaching program is run in a group forum for six2-hour sessions over a 2-day period.

The program presents a fantastic way to improve both the parents' and the youths' futures.

To claim your free bonuses, please visit
www.TheYouthEvolution.com

ABOUT THE AUTHOR

Yetunde Juliet Adeshile MBA, MAPM, BSc

Yetunde is a sought after coach, public speaker and consultant who has the passion for seeing youths achieve purpose and destiny. She strongly believes that mentoring and coaching can help in focusing the minds of the next generation for success. It is also her belief that focusing the minds of youths will lead to an increase in their capability to achieve greater success, which in turn may lead to better social behaviours, reduced crime rate, teenage pregnancy, unemployment, killings, poverty and time wasting among youths.

Yetunde is the founder and CEO of The Next Chosen Generation (TNCG CIC). This is an organisation that delivers mentoring and coaching for youths as well as parent coaching in order to help them achieve purpose and succeed in life. Yetunde also volunteers as a STEM Ambassador for schools in the UK. This voluntary role means that she goes into UK schools to provide career guidance, motivational speaking, mentoring and coaching support to children in secondary schools. She has been doing this for over seven years.

She has also volunteered as a mentor to teens with the AWE School Mentor Programme in Berkshire. The experience and results she has achieved demonstrates that, with the right mentoring and coaching support, youths can achieve better results in all aspects of their lives.

Yetunde has served in various youth ministries for over 20 years. She currently serves as the youth pastor at the Redeemed Christian Church of God (RCCG) The Fountain Parish UK, and has held this position for over three years.

Yetunde is also the Director of RJ Emmanuel Ltd. A Management Consultancy that specialises in Project Management, Internet Marketing and Publishing & Promotions Consultancy.

About the Author

She is married to Mr. Peter Olatunde Adeshile and between them they have three children: Rachael, James, and Emmanuel.

Yetunde is a dynamic speaker with the ability to challenge and inspire the audience to focus on what really matters for their success through her experience and story.

To find out more about Yetunde's keynote presentations, workshops and personal appearances, you can contact her at:

Yetunde Adeshile
The Next Chosen Generation
The Laindon Barn
Dunton Road
Basildon
Essex
SS15 4DB

Phone: 01268 330029
Fax: 01268 330742
Email: yetunde@yetundeadeshile.com
Web Address: www.yetundeadeshile.com
Connect on Facebook: Yetunde Juliet Adeshile
Follow on Twitter: @y_adeshile
Link up on LinkedIn: Yetunde Adeshile

ACKNOWLEDGMENTS

"But in a great house there are not only vessels of gold and of silver, but also of wood and of earth; and some of honour, and some of dishonour." **2 Timothy 2:21**

I would not be the person I am today, and therefore this book may never have been written without the love of God. For affording me with the privilege to be used as a vessel of honour in His vineyard. For trusting me with His next generation. For giving me a heart that yearns for the next generation, to see them succeed and achieve their full potential.

To all my spiritual parents who helped me to hold on to the faith and lift my spirits through their events, TV programmes, service and books. Pastor E A Adeboye, Pastor (Mrs) F Adeboye, Pastor. Agu Iruku, Pastor Mathew Ashimolowo, Bishop TD Jakes, Pastor (Mrs) Y Ashimolowo, Joyce Meyer Ministries, Pastor (Mrs) Funke Felix-Adejumo, Dr. Cindy Trimm and all other great men of God that are doing great works for His kingdom.

To Pastor Thomas Aderounmu and Pastor (Mrs) Elizabeth Aderounmu for obeying God's instructions and entrusting me with RCCG The Fountain – The Chosen Youth Church. For standing on the trust and teaching God's word as it is.

To Pastor John Addison and Mrs. Christine Addison, for your spiritual mentorship and guidance. For giving me the platform to express the gift that God has deposited in me.

To Pastor Michael Sasere and Deaconess Meru Olaoshebikan of RCCG The Fountain. For your love and supporting me to remain focused on God's purpose for me in ministry.

To all the great leaders out there that are helping people like me to reach our full potentials and making us know that the sky is truly the limit, Pastor Shola Adeaga and all the mentors on the Esther's mentoring scheme (RCCG Jesus House), Lisa Nichols, John Lee, Andy Harrington, Simon Coulson and Coaches at The Coaching Academy,

Acknowledgments

To my International Educational Coach and Mentor, Mrs. Yemisi Akindele. For all you have done, doing and will continue to do. Thank you.

To Pastor Samuel Adeagbo Adeshile, Oluwabunmi Oriade, Ajiboye Adeshile and the entire Adeshile family for your support and encouragement. I appreciate and love you all.

To my siblings, Big Sis. Titiloye Ashamu, Omotunde Victor Ashamu, Temitope Ashamu and Oyetayo Nuga. For always being there for me whenever I need your support. Thank you for your care and unconditional love always.

To my book mentor, Richard McMann, and all the staff at how-2-become, especially Jordan Cooke and Joshua Brown who project managed this project from start to finish. Thank you for all your support and patience and putting up with all my changes.

To my book writing and marketing coach Gerry Roberts. Your training and coaching definitely gave me the confidence that I could write this book. It also brought to light the many opportunities that this would lead to. Thank you for the testimonial as well.

To my book coach, Christine Kloser through her *Get Your Book Done Home Study Course;* without you, I would still be pregnant with this book inside of me. Thank you for the advertising platform as well.

To Raymond Aaron for writing the foreword of this book and his 10-10-10 programme that gave me the network and platform that eliminated procrastination, thus enabling me to complete this book in a very short space of time. Many thanks to all the staff and authors of the 10-10-10 programme, especially Vishal Morjaria, Naval Kumar and Lisa Browning.

To all my friends, family and in-laws especially Mrs. Abosede Fayehun and Mrs. Oluwatoyin Mayugbe for your continued support and love always. I love you all dearly.

To my author partners, who made sure that I never settled down for less Oluwaseun Oke and Oladunni Owo, I will forever remain grateful to God for giving us the opportunity to meet and take this wonderful journey together. I appreciate you both.

To book reviewers Eanas El Sheakh, Carole Pyke and Karen Small. Thank you for taking your time to review the content of this book. Thank you for your honest feedback. You are very much appreciated.

To the RCCG the Fountain - The Chosen Youth, especially the leadership team Samuel Aderounmu, Adeola Alaran and Victoria Aderounmu. You are my first teachers in this ministry. You may not know it, but being your youth pastor is what has yielded this fruit. I love you all always.

To The Next Chosen Generation (TNCG), parents, caretakers and youth members. For attending TNCG sessions, for being bold, supportive, dedicated and for trusting me to be your mentor and coach.

To the 'Awesomettes'. For putting procrastinating about writing this book in the past. You guys are awesome.

To Olabisi Olatunji, for your support, encouragement and faithfulness.

To Funke Michael for your support and encouragement. You are highly appreciated.

To my children, Rachael, James and Emmanuel for your love. You keep me pressing on to greater heights. For always supporting, encouraging and believing in your mum. I love you all to the moon and back.

To my husband Peter Olatunde Adeshile. My solid rock. For giving me the freedom to do everything that God has asked me to do. For always being there for me. For your love, care and support. You are one of a kind and you are mine forever and always.

BIBLIOGRAPHY

UNESCO. *What Do We Mean by "Youth?" UNESCO Social and Human Sciences,* Youth, [online] Available at: http://www.unesco.org/new/en/social-and-human-sciences/themes/youth/youth-definition/ [accessed 12 July, 2015].

UN (2015). *Definition of Youth* [online] Available at: http://www.un.org/esa/socdev/documents/youth/fact-sheets/youth-definition.pdf [Accessed 12 July. 2015].

Kennedy, R. (1966). *Day of Affirmation Address.* Speech in Capetown, South Africa (6 June 1966).

McCridle, M. (2015). *The Generation Map.* [Online] Available at: http://McCridle.com.au/resources/whitepapers/McCrindle-Research_ABC-03_The-Generation-Map_Mark-McCrindle.pdf [Accessed 19 July. 2015].

The Independent, (2014). *The online generation: Four in 10 children are addicted to the internet.* [Online] Available at: http://www.independent.co.uk/life-style/gadgets-and-tech/news/the-online-generation-four-in-10-children-are-addicted-to-the-internet-9341159.html [Accessed 20 July. 2015].

Nidirect.gov.uk, (2014). *Enjoy the internet safely: Click Clever, Click Safe | indirect.* [online] Available at: http://www.nidirect.gov.uk/enjoy-the-internet-safely-click-clever-click-safe [Accessed 14 Jul. 2015].

The Confederation of British Industry, A New Approach for our schools, 2012 Report

Jakes T.D, Instincts, 2012

Meyer J, Overcoming Fear with faith, Audio Teaching 2014

Maxwell, J. (2011). *Put your dream to the test.* Nashville: Thomas Nelson, Inc.

Covey, S. (2004). *The 7 habits of highly effective people.* New York: Free Press.

Pegues, D. (2011). *30 Days to Taming Your Fears: Practical Help for a More Peaceful and Productive Life.* Eugene, Oregon: Harvest House Publishers.

Adeboye EA, Open Heavens, 2013

The Coaching Academy (2015), Training Materials

Word for Today (2015)

Malcolm X, Goodreads.com, (September 2015)

Mother Teresa, Goodreads.com, (August 2015)

Einstine A, Quotesjunk.com, August 2015

Oxford Dictionaries, www.oxforddictionaries.com, August 2015

CCPAS Setting Standards in Safeguarding (2011), *Safeguarding in a digital world*

Cambridge International Examinations (Website), 2015

Thomas Nelson, The Woman's Study Bible – Second Edition, New King James Version, 2006

RECOMMENDED RESOURCES

How to Succeed as a Parent – Steve Chalke, Hodder & Stoughton

How to Succeed as a Working Parent - Steve Chalke, Hodder & Stoughton

How to Talk So Kids Will Listen and Listen So Kids Will Talk – Adele Faber

Who Moved My Cheese – Dr. Spencer Johnson (dealing with change)

The Psychology of Judgment and Decision Making (McGraw-Hill Series in Social Psychology)

Smart Choices: A Practical Guide to Making Better Decisions – John S. Hammond, Ralph L. Keeney, Howard Raiffa

Foluke Sangobowale, *11+ Exams Parent's Get A Grip,* 2014

Covey S, 1998, *The 7 Habits of Highly Effective TEENS*

USEFUL WEBSITES

www.goggle.com   This is a very useful search engine, for any topic that you may want to research.

www.bbc.co.uk

www.vodaphone.com/parents

www.virginstartup.org

www.gov.uk

www.princes-trust.org.uk

www.ingramcontent.com/pod-product-compliance
Lightning Source LLC
Chambersburg PA
CBHW050644160426
43194CB00010B/1806